How to Deliver Client/Server Applications That Work

How to Deliver Client/Server Applications That Work

ALEX BAKMAN

MANNING

Greenwich

The publisher offers discounts on this book when ordered in quantity. For more information, please contact:

Special Sales Department
Manning Publications Co.
3 Lewis Street
Greenwich, CT 06830

Fax: (203) 661-9018
email: 73150.1431@compuserve.com

Recognizing the importance of preserving what has been written, it is the policy of Manning to have the books they publish printed on acid-free paper, and we exert our best efforts to that end.

Library of Congress Cataloging-in-Publication Data
Bakman, Alex, 1965–
        How to deliver client/server applications that work / Alex Bakman.
            p.   cm.
        Includes index.
        ISBN 1-884777-04-X
        1. Client/server computing.   2. Application software.   I. Title.
    QA76.9.C55B34   1995
    005.2—dc20
                                                        94-39133
                                                            CIP

 Manning Publications Co.
3 Lewis Street
Greenwich, CT 06830

Design: Frank Cunningham
Copyeditor: Margaret Marynowski
Typesetter: Aaron Lyon

Printed in the United States of America
1 2 3 4 5 6 7 8 9 10 - BB - 98 97 96 95

Contents

II
Distributed Systems Technology

III
Application Development and Deployment

Preface

Client/server technology will undoubtedly become the dominant computing paradigm in the 1990s and will remain so into the twenty-first century. The pressure toward greater business efficiency, increased productivity, and continuous cost reduction necessitates that a multitude of computers, both large and small, be integrated into a scalable, cost-effective computing solution. This integration must blend all systems into a seamless computing resource, where network and application boundaries no longer exist.

Users will benefit from this integration, as it will allow them to gain more control over their data. This will inevitably lessen their dependency on information system organizations for many routine data access needs. Users will be able to improve their productivity, and the information system group will be able to focus its resources on assembling the building blocks of a corporate computing infrastructure.

The road to successful client/server computing is not an easy one. It requires an unprecedented level of cooperation between a business and its information system organization. Such cooperation must be expressed through mutual understanding, coordinated planning, and open communication. In addition to the business challenges of client/server computing, many technical challenges remain. The lack of good systems management tools, limits to tool scalability, and difficulties in using tools remain significant obstacles.

This book examines the business and technical challenges of client/server computing. Its aim is to help the reader through all the stages of a client/server project, from conceptualization to system deployment, while giving practical information in a concise manner.

ALEX BAKMAN

CleverSoft Inc.
Portland, Maine

Acknowledgments

I would like to take this opportunity to thank the individuals and organizations who have helped me in this endeavor. First, I would like to thank many of my colleagues at UNUM Life Insurance company for their encouragement and support, in particular, Paul Selsky, Randy Chapman, Rick Hebert, Dan Charest-Berglove, Mark Sontz, Scott Sanford, and Tom Liao. I would also like to thank Emil Ansarov of ObjectKnowledge, Al Mak of Goldman Sachs, Rich Schreiber of ATB Associates, Scott Lyon of Target Stores, and Pete Koolish for their feedback and review. A special thanks to my publisher, Marjan Bace for his support, encouragement, and guidance. And last but not least, a huge thanks goes to my family—Alexandra, Sarah, and Benjamin—for their support and patience.

1

Introduction

American businesses are experiencing an unprecedented amount of change, and more than ever, they are looking to computer technology for solutions to challenges.

Distributed computing technology has found its way into almost every aspect of such technological solutions, and yet knowledge of how to apply it correctly is still scarce. This general lack of knowledge leads to projects that fail, tarnished reputations, and broken careers. In many instances, such failure is perceived as failure of the technology.

The aim of this book is to provide practical information on how to apply distributed computing technology successfully. The book is essentially a roadmap to delivering distributed systems. It starts with the conceptualization of a system and goes through the various stages of design, development, and implementation.

Whom is This Book For?

As someone involved in the application of distributed computing technology, I found it difficult to locate practical information on such applications. Most books fall into two broad categories: the first class of books describes distributed computing technology from a "fifty thousand foot" level, without much technical detail. These books are primarily targeted at executives, to help them with strategic decision making.

Another class of books on distributed computing is aimed at the programmer. Such books are often many hundreds of pages long, and are filled with an incredible amount of technical detail. However, they give very little nontechnical advice.

Many hours spent on synthesizing information from both kinds of sources have convinced me that there is a need for a book to help those of us responsible for delivering distributed systems. If you are a project leader, a project manager, a system architect, a chief programmer, or someone who wants to learn practical information on how to deliver distributed system solutions, this book is for you. It will help you to deal with the business and management issues, and to examine many architectural and design challenges of building distributed systems, and provide you with concrete and practical technical advice.

How to Read This Book

I have structured this book to reflect the sequence of steps that one follows in delivering a distributed system solution. The book consists of three parts. Part I addresses management and business issues. It deals with the difficult, but absolutely crucial question of whether distributed technology is applicable to the business problem at hand. It offers suggestions on how to promote the use of client/server technology to users and management. It examines the benefits and challenges of distributed technology. Finally, some suggestions are given for vendor management and for organizing project teams.

Part II focuses on the technical aspects of distributed technology. Chapter 6 conceptualizes distributed system technology in the form of a road map. Building on that chapter, Chapter 7 demonstrates the most frequently used models for building distributed systems.

Part III offers a methodology for building and managing client/server systems. This section starts out by demonstrating how object-oriented analyses and design can be applied to client/server development. Distributed systems testing and deployment are subsequently explored. Chapter 13 presents various software distribution techniques, organizational support structures, distributed systems management tools and techniques, and other important implementation issues.

The information in this book generally falls into three groups:

- Business and management issues

- Technical architecture and design issues

- Technical detail and implementation issues

While some readers are interested in all three issues, others might prefer to skip around. The reader is encouraged to explore only those sections that are of real interest.

Terminology

The computer industry is notorious for its lack of consistent terminology, and distributed computing is no exception. Before we proceed, let's define the most common terms that will be used in this book. I realize that you may have come across a different set of meanings, but in order for us to understand each other let's use these terms as they are defined here.

Let's define some common terminology

The word *distributed* means that a system involves more than one computer. When a system consists of many components that run on different computers it is said to be a distributed system. For example, a network operating system such as Microsoft's LAN Manager is certainly a distributed system, because it consists of a client component which runs on every users' machine and server components (Figure 1.1).

A distributed systems involves more than one computer

A common misconception in the industry is that distributed applications involve only workstations and personal computers. Many distributed systems are PC-based, but the term encompasses many other types of computers, including mini computers and large mainframes.

Distributed systems encompass all types of computers

**Figure 1.1   Example of a
distributed system: MS LAN
Manager**

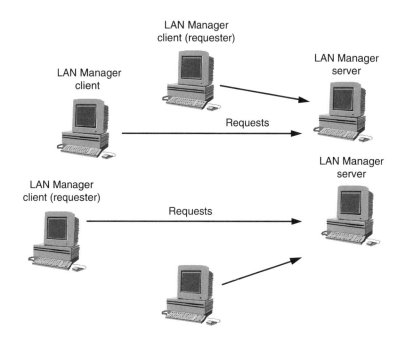

LAN Manager
client (requester)

LAN Manager
server

LAN Manager
client

Requests

LAN Manager
server

LAN Manager
client (requester)

Requests

Client/Server Computing

*The phrases client/server
and distributed will
mean roughly the same
thing*

Over the last several years, a popular phrase has emerged in the press
and in the vendor community. The phrase *client/server computing* is
now synonymous with almost any form of distributed computing.
Therefore for consistency, I will use the phrases *client/server* and *distributed systems* somewhat interchangeably.

*Client/server computing
encompasses a wide
array of system solutions*

Many people mistakenly associate client/server computing only with
database applications. Essentially, any database application that sends
SQL requests across the network to a DBMS server is called a client/
server application. This type of an application is certainly an example
of a client/server database application, but the client/server model has
a much broader definition which extends beyond database
applications.

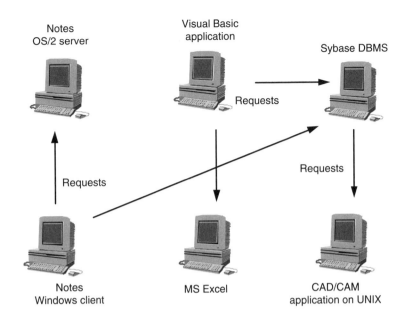

Figure 1.2   A client/server relationship can exist between many diverse systems

First and foremost, client/server is a computing model, where one application (the client) sends requests to another application (the server) for processing. For example, in Figure 1.2, a Lotus Notes Windows application (client) sends requests to a Notes server on OS/2, which processes them and replies to the client. As already mentioned, a client/server application does not necessarily need to be a database application. For example, a network operating system such as Novell's NetWare is a client/server system. A NetWare client component called the Netware shell sends I/O read and write requests to a Netware file server, which processes them (Figure 1.3).

The client/server designation is not a physical attribute, but a role that an application takes on at a particular point in time. For example, an application can be a client in one instance and a server in another.

A client/server model is a form of a master/slave relationship. The server would never send unsolicited requests to a client. The client initiates all such requests to the server, and the server merely replies.

A client component always sends requests, and servers reply

Client/server is a role

The client initiates all requests

Figure 1.3   Client/server interaction in Netware

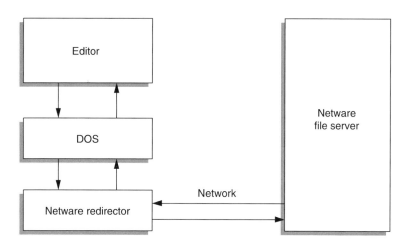

Cooperative Processing

Cooperative *means more than one software component*

When a system consists of two or more independent components that run on different machines, we say that it exhibits *cooperative processing*. The distributed components cooperate with each other in order to accomplish some user task.

Figure 1.4   Peer-to-peer relationship

Cooperative processing is synonymous with the term *peer-to-peer*. In a peer-to-peer system, all components of a distributed system are equal peers and can send requests to each other for processing (Figure 1.4). Unlike the client/server relationship, any peer can send and perform requests; i.e., no one peer is designated to be a server at all times.

In a peer-to-peer system, any component can send requests to other components

You can think of each peer as being both a client and a server. In this model, every peer must be ready to receive requests from other peers.

Peers are both clients and servers

State of the Industry

In many respects, distributed computing technology is still in its infancy. This is not to say that distributed technology is not ready to be used at this time. On the contrary, those who have used it successfully have achieved remarkable benefits. The real challenges are to know when distributed technology should be applied and how to apply it correctly. The goal of this book is to address these fundamental questions.

How to apply distributed technology correctly is what this book is about

Suggested Reading

Alex Berson, *Client/Server Architecture,* New York: McGraw-Hill, 1992.

Patrick Smith, *Client/Server Computing,* Carmel, IN: SAMS Publishing, 1992.

Dick Conklin, ed., *OS/2 Notebook,* Redmond, WA: Microsoft Press, 1990.

2

To Proceed or Not to Proceed

In this chapter we will deal with the difficult, but absolutely crucial issue of how to decide whether a project should make use of distributed technology. Certainly, if there are overwhelming reasons not to proceed, the right time to discover them is at an early stage, while investments are low.

My goal in this chapter is to focus your attention on important business and technical issues in order to help you make this decision. Not all of the issues discussed here will be applicable to your project, but I hope that at least some will be and that others will give you "food for thought."

The decision to implement a system is not trivial, regardless of which technology is used. There are many factors involved, some of which will be totally outside of your control. By staying on top of business and technical issues, you can improve your chances of success.

Management Support

Before you proceed with any project involving new technology, you should be confident that you have your management's support. As with any new technology, the lack of management support will often result in canceled projects and inadequate funds, and will label the individual who spearheaded the effort as a *heat seeker,* a corporate term for an individual who is not politically smart and jumps in on any new technology.

Management support is a must

In order to win support for your project from management, you must be able to convince them of its merit. A good way to do that is through a cost/benefit analysis. A thorough analysis should take most of the guesswork out of the decision making process.

A cost benifit analysis helps to make a rational business decision

Solid management support will assure funding	No matter how well you plan ahead, a distributed system's project will likely exceed its budget. There are many unpredictable obstacles for which you simply can't account. Going back for additional resources should always be an open option.

Get a Client Sponsor

Find a client who needs a business problem solved	Every successful project starts with an unfulfilled need. Focusing on addressing that need is a great step in the right direction. Present your idea to an important client of your company. He or she will bring legitimacy to your project, help you promote the project, and give you a head start toward creating a good working relationship between the development team and its end users. The importance of getting a sponsor cannot be emphasized enough.
The sponsor should be a respected business person	A good place to look for such a sponsor is in the business community which will use the system. The best choice of a sponsor would be somebody who can fund the project, or minimally, someone who can place the project on an equal footing with other projects in the management's review.

Start Simple, Start Small

Keep your first project technically as simple as possible	When implementing your first distributed system, the best advice that can be given is, *start simple and start small.* You must do all you can to minimize risk. There are at least two sources of risk that you should be cognizant of—technology and business.
Select an existing application to redo with this new technology	In order to minimize the business risk, it is better to select a business domain with which you are already familiar. One possibility is to improve an existing application or a subset of it. For example, on a recent project we recognized that replacing an existing mainframe system with a new distributed system was not only risky but costly. The decision was made to develop only a subset of the system to run in a local area network. The particular subset was chosen because it would make good use of the LAN environment and provide the most value to our users.

Another advantage to selecting a subset of a existing system is that you can be confident that the problem you are trying to solve is a legitimate one. That should help you strengthen your case with the management.

This will help ensure that you are focusing on a needed solution

Get Users on Your Side

Another way to reduce the business risk is to make sure that you have commitment to the project from business users. As with any new technology, the business users will deliver the final judgment on the usefulness of a system, which often translates into a verdict for technology. Be sure that your business users have dedicated a reasonable amount of time to work on this project with you. This not only demonstrates their commitment to the project, but also distributes the sense of ownership and responsibility for delivering the system to all parties involved.

You must develop a strong relationship with your users

As systems people, we sometimes loose sight of how important a particular system is to the business. This can lead to being overly ambitious in applying new and unproven technology. While the business users might appear excited about the new technology, you must know your user's level of tolerance when things don't work out as well as desired.

Know the boundaries of this relationship

In order to get a better idea of the importance of your project, try to classify it as either mission critical or non-mission critical—put another way, systems that are *the business* and those that are *about the business*. The distinction is fairly obvious. Users will typically have low tolerance for down time of systems that are the business, because of their criticality to the functions of the business. For example, a bank would be unable to conduct its operations if its customer account information system were unavailable. Users would probably have a much greater tolerance for down time of other systems, such as systems for human resources management.

Classify the project as mission critical or non-mission critical

By selecting a system that is about the business, you gain some "breathing space," which you will surely come to appreciate in the later stages of the project. The disadvantage is that you probably

There are advantages and disadvantages to both types of projects

won't receive as much attention in terms of funding and recognition as with business-critical projects.

Strike a Balance

Strive to balance technology risks with their business value

In considering technical issues, you should try to strike a balance between being overly conservative, by not taking advantage of technology that can bring significant business benefits, and being overly aggressive, by using unproven technology.

An example of a balanced risk

As an example, consider implementing a system which requires the use of multiple databases located at different physical sites. Let's assume that the databases need to be tightly synchronized. This task might require a lot of complicated code, and the opportunity for failure could be fairly high. Your goal should be to try and simplify the design of the system without sacrificing the business benefits. Maybe in this example, it would be possible to find a database management system (DBMS) which offers built-in replication services, and thus avoid developing new code alltogether.

Good Team = Success

The team is your most important asset

One of the first questions that I hope you ask yourself is, "Does my team have the necessary skills and experience to implement the new system?" Regardless of which technology is used, the team, or more specifically, the technical skills, experience, and dedication of its members, will make or break the project.

You might have to compromise

If the team does not have the necessary skills you will have to either make the project fit their skills or make their skills fit the project. Put another way, you will either have to implement a solution which can be accomplished with the skills your team already has or have the team acquire new ones. Gaining skills and experience takes time and money.

A knowledgable consulatant can be very helpful…

If you are working under a tight deadline, especially on a highly visible project, you can get a lot of mileage by bringing in an experienced consultant. A successful consulting engagement would not only help you deliver the system on time and on budget, but also transfer the knowledge and experience to your team.

A knowledgeable consultant can serve as a project mentor. He or she can help with the initial design, identify appropriate education for team members, and contribute experience in a particular product or a set of products. This experience can help the team get around known product limitations, thus saving the time and effort needed to build a system.

…and cost effective

Now, let's focus on important technical issues that need to be factored into every distributed system decision.

Decision Support or Transaction Processing

Another important issue is the type of the intended system. Generally speaking, most systems fall into two broad categories—decision support and transaction processing.

Distributed systems are either decision support or transaction processing

A typical decision support system, as the name implies, helps users in their decision-making processes. A decision support system is not an operational system used in daily business activities. Instead, it allows users to examine accumulated business data in many ways. A good decision support system has a *drill down* capability, which helps users zoom in on a particular piece of data, or zoom out to show broad trends. An example of a decision support system could be an executive information system, which provides executives with vital business data on the company's performance.

The goal of the decision support systems is to improve decision making

Generally speaking, distributed decision support systems are easier to implement than operational, transaction oriented systems. First of all, decision support systems do not normally modify data, and that reduces complexity. Second, users work with decision support systems less frequently than with operational systems, and that reduces problems with multiple users trying to access the same data concurrently.

Decision support systems are easier to implement than transaction processing systems

Finally, the users of decision support systems are more tolerant to slow response times. They understand that aggregating the data and performing the "What if…?" analyses takes time.

The speed of decision support systems is less important than other factors

Conversely, transaction processing systems must be fast

In contrast, users are very sensitive when their transaction processing system does not respond instantly! The reason is that users are expected to perform hundreds, and possibly thousands, of transactions per day. The last thing they want is a system that slows them down.

Therefore, distributed transaction processing systems are more difficult to build

Distributed transaction processing systems are much more difficult to build than are decision support systems. The complexity associated with database concurrency, instant response time expectations, and resource synchronization issues make distributed transaction systems a real implementation challenge.

An airline reservation system is an example of a high end transaction processing system

An extreme example of a high end transaction processing system is an airline reservation system. Just imagine trying to provide subsecond system response time to thousands of users simultaneously accessing the system from locations worldwide!

Try to build transaction processing systems with a single data source

If you choose to build a transactional system, try to simplify the application design with a single physical database. Having a single database will take away the need for a two-phase commit protocol and will remove much of the application complexity associated with it.

Figure 2.1 System transactions in a multisite distributed system

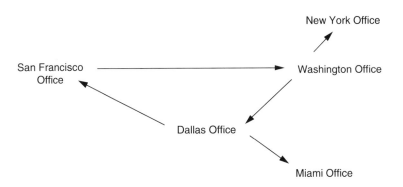

Data synchronization and integrity are difficult to achieve if data are distributed

Consider this simple, but realistic example. You are asked to implement a transaction processing system for users located in multiple field offices, who must be able to share data (Figure 2.1). There is a very natural temptation to design the system using multiple physical databases: the main corporate database and a separate database in each field office. As the users update the data, the changes need to be simultaneously reflected in the local field office database and in the main corporate database. What if a transaction succeeds in a local database, but fails in the corporate database? The result could lead to data integrity problems.

A transaction oriented system must be able to coordinate transactions with multiple resource managers, in this case DBMSs, and must be able to back out of the changes issued to all if one fails. This type of coordination in distributed systems is still in its infancy.

Data synchronization technology is still immature

Many system developers believe that they need a local database, because of slow wide area network connections. With the cost of communication lines decreasing, it might be cheaper to upgrade the speed of your connections or to redesign your application architecture and stay with a single database solution, than to have many local databases. This is especially true if the quantity of data that crosses the communication lines is relatively small. If the quantity of data is large, you can make use of highly effective data compression/decompression libraries. It is much easier to upgrade the speed of communication lines than to deal with complex and error-prone applications logic.

Reexamine your application architecture or purchase faster links to improve speed

System Size

Another important factor to consider is the number of users that your distributed system will have to support. Naturally, as the number of users on the system increases so does its complexity. A typical problem associated with a large number of users is the contention for data within the database engine.

System size is an impotant issue

A traditional database management system controls user access to data by implementing a variety of locking schemes. For example, if one user is updating a customer table, the database will lock out other users from making changes to that table. As the number of users grows, these built-in locking mechanisms become problematic. In a complex application, the data access control is best handled in the application code. By analyzing the user access patterns, a better access control approach can be devised.

Database contention issues can be better addressed at the applications level

Network speeds are still the bottleneck of distributed systems

The network traffic will proportionally increase with the number of users of your system. It is a good idea to estimate the quantity of data and the traffic patterns before finishing the physical design. The networks are still the slowest part of any distributed system.

There is a significant difference in speed between internal and network connections

Consider the differences between the internal processor-to-memory access speeds (10 Meg/sec) or processor-to-I/O speed (roughly 1 Meg/sec), and the network. A typical 4-megabit/second token ring network has a theoretical throughput of about 400 kilobytes per second. A more realistic number after the overhead of the communication layers is subtracted is on the order of 100 to 200 kilobytes per second. That is at least an order of the magnitude slower than internal computer speeds! Therefore, you must pay particular attention to how your application uses the network.

Is it a WAN or LAN Application?

Today's LAN applications do not scale to run on a corporate-wide network

Many local area networks started out as departmental connectivity solutions. It didn't take long for users to start demanding connectivity to other departmental LANs. Thus, virtual LANs, possibly spanning entire continents, were born. The problem is that a good number of LAN applications do not scale well to this environment.

Wide area network bridges connecting slow wide area links often become congested

Consider this example. Let's assume that we have bridged together two local area networks—one in Chicago and another in Los Angeles —with a 56-Kbps bridge (Figure 2.2). Such a bridge roughly delivers a 5-Kbps pipe between the two LANs. As soon as the traffic in the network increases, the bridge becomes a bottleneck.

If an application is to run in a wide area network, it must take these slow wide area links into consideration

Chances are that the users won't be very happy with this system's performance. You must be able to anticipate the network speeds under which a system will have to execute and to select the most appropriate application architecture for it.

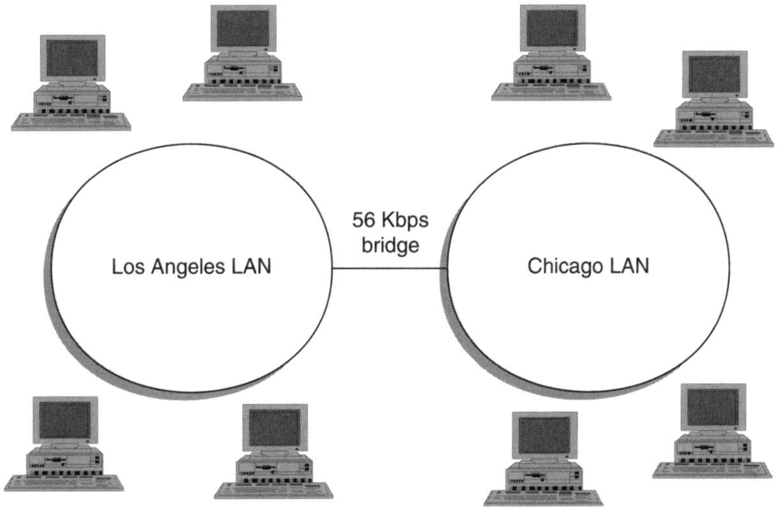

Figure 2.2   Bridged LANs

56 Kbps bridge

Los Angeles LAN

Chicago LAN

The Geography

The geographic locations of your users is also important in terms of being able to manage a system. It is much easier to support a system which has all of its users in one building than one having multiple sites around the world. If this is the first distributed system in the company, the support tools, procedures, and organization needed might prove to be technically and financially challenging.

Having users at multiple geographic sites adds complexity in systems management

The tools currently available for remote application control, software distribution, configuration, and other management tasks are just beginning to emerge and still lack significant functionality. Realistically speaking, the support of distributed applications today is very labor intensive.

Lack of tools makes this effort very labor intensive

Importance of Proper Application Architecture

Selecting the right application architecture is another important factor. By application *architecture,* I mean the physical partitioning of your application into client and server components. In a centralized system, poor application architecture can usually be corrected by add-

Proper application architecture is even more important in distributed systems

ing more hardware. This approach can bring only marginal improvements to a distributed system.

The architecture has a lot to do with scalability of a system and its performance

In the distributed applications world, how you partition the system will affect the system's ability to scale with the number of users, determine its performance, and set a precedent for how this system will interact with other systems in the company. In short, a distributed system must be designed to be scalable. When designed correctly, a distributed system should be able to support three hundred users just as efficiently as ten (Figure 2.3).

Figure 2.3 Distributed application architecture

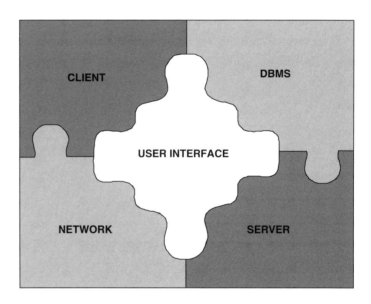

Today's generation of client/server tools lacks architectural flexibility

You should be wary of tools that impose a certain architecture on your system: the majority of the client/server tools available today are not really client/server, but just client tools. Such tools allow you to build front ends (client components) to a back end DBMS. Since the entire application runs on every user's machine and your application code is not really distributed among machines in the network, your users will need more powerful desktop machines.

Enterprise-wide distributed systems cannot be built with the existing toolset

The inability to distribute processing using this application architecture prevents it from being scalable. This architecture will serve well for simple applications, but as your application grows in size and complexity it will likely become problematic.

Scale—Departmental or Enterprise Wide?

Implementing distributed systems on a large scale can be extremely challenging. It is no surprise that the majority of distributed systems built to date have tended to be departmental rather than enterprise wide. An enterprise-wide system serves multiple divisions of a company and typically has users in many different departments. In addition, an enterprise-wide system is likely to have users at multiple geographic sites.

Enterprise-wide systems have many users at numerous sites

In contrast, a departmental system has most of its users in one location. Its users perform similar functions. Naturally, departmental systems are easier to develop and manage. Keeping a distributed system within a particular division or department is somewhat like keeping it in the family. You will typically find a more understanding audience during the *growing pains*. Having users locally will reduce the need for expensive systems management tools.

Enterprise-wide systems are more difficult to build and manage

Operational Support

You must also think beyond the system development stage and clearly formulate your vision regarding the operational support of a system in production. It is a very common mistake to concentrate solely on the system development issues without addressing the operational side of things. In fact, operational support is likely to be just as challenging as building a system. Operational support consists of procedures, tools, and defining responsibilities. It will be addressed in much greater detail later in the book.

Operational support must not be taken lightly

The following list of questions is meant to help you make an assessment of your proposed system and to bring out important factors for further considerations. If you find yourself giving many *yes* responses, some red flags should go up. I am not suggesting canceling projects, but simply want to alert you to areas that could be problematic.

Questions to ask yourself before proceeding

1   Will the system support over 60 users?

2   Will the system deliver new functionality to the business?

3   Will you use a new programming language or an application development tool?

4   Will a LAN-based DBMS contain over 2 gigabytes of data?

5   Will the system experience a high transaction rate (over 20 transactions per second)?

6   Will the system require a new hardware base?

7   Will the system require a new operating system, DBMS, or communications software?

8   Will the system have multiple databases on different machines?

9   Will the system provide 2–3-second response time 80% of the time?

10 Will users be located at multiple geographic sites?

11 Will it take over a year to build this system?

12 Does your staff lack the design and programming skills needed to implement this system?

13 Will the system serve multiple departments with different functions?

14 Are there frequent local or wide area network problems in your company?

15 Is there a lack of qualified skills in the company to support distributed systems?

16 Is there a lack of procedures for problem resolution on distributed systems?

17 Is there a lack of support organization for distributed systems?

18 Are you lacking the tools needed to support distributed systems in production?

Conclusion

The decision to build a distributed system is not simple. It must be reviewed in light of business and management objectives. It must also be technologically feasible. In the next chapter, we will examine how to examine such a decision from a financial point of view. The costs and benefits of client/server systems will be examined in more detail, creating a general framework which can be applied to many client/server projects.

"It is better to measure seven times and cut only once"*

Suggested Reading

W. H. Inmon, *Developing Client/Server Applications,* Boston: QED Technical Publishing, 1991.

Shaku Atre, *Distributed Databases, Cooperative Processing and Networking,* New York: McGraw-Hill, 1992.

"Transaction Processing," *DBMS Magazine,* December 1990.

---

* Russian proverb

3

Cost/Benefit Analysis of Client/Server Systems

How many times have you wondered whether a project was really worth the effort? Well, you are not alone. In talking to my colleagues around the country, I was shocked to learn how often multimillion dollar projects get started without clearly articulated business objectives!

Every business decision should always be financially sound. This principle must be applied to all business activities, including systems development projects. Before any business commits to spending potentially a large amount of money to build a system, it must justify its decision through a financial analysis technique called cost/benefit analysis.

Cost/benefit analysis is examined in this chapter in the context of distributed systems. My challenge is to help you correctly identify the expenses and the benefits of distributed systems. Without a good understanding of these factors, a cost/benefit analysis is of little use.

The Mechanics of Cost/Benefit Analysis

First, let's explain how cost/benefit analysis is computed. While there are many financial ways to compute a cost/benefit analysis (e.g., taking into account net present value), the fundamentals are the same. Put simply, cost/benefit analysis is performed by adding the benefits of a proposed system and subtracting the expenses. If the difference is a positive number, the project makes good financial sense:

ALL BENEFITS − ALL COSTS = RETURN ON INVESTMENT (ROI)

Mechanics of cost/benefit analysis

In the simplest scenario, projects are chosen solely based on their ROI value. For example, if there are two competing projects, one offering $120,000 ROI and another $200,000, the latter gets picked.

In reality many other factors affect the decision making process. For example, a company might be particularly interested in receiving a short term benefit and choose the project that delivers the quickest return, as opposed to the largest total return. Often, a project with a relatively low ROI gets picked on the merits of its strategic value. The bottom line is, just because the initial numbers don't look encouraging, does not mean that your project is not worth pursuing.

The Biggest Client/Server Myth

The biggest myth of client/server applications is that they cost less than their mainframe equivalents. Surely, when the comparison is made based solely on the cost of millions of instructions per second (MIPS), there is a huge gap in favor of client/server systems, but MIPS alone do *not* tell the whole story. It is only when the total implementation costs are considered, that an apples-to-apples comparison can be made.

Many early adapters of distributed technology are finding that some client/server systems can actually cost more! One study, for example, has concluded that a $2,500 personal computer costs a company over $40,000 per year to maintain. As you will see later in the book when we cover training, support, software distribution, additional tools, and other costs, the expense does become quite substantial.

The justification for building client/server systems comes not from savings in information systems (IS) expenditure, but from increases in user productivity, from job elimination, or from gaining a competitive advantage.

Expenses, Expenses, and More Expenses

Let's now examine the sources of networked applications' expenses. The most obvious is the cost of hardware. This includes computers, network adapters, network wiring, bridges, and routers. Don't forget to include the labor cost of wiring a site. This item can be prohibitively expensive, especially in many older buildings and highly unionized cities, like New York. The table below should give you an idea of what the hardware costs are.

Wiring	About $200 per cable/per user for an unshielded twisted pair used for token ring networks. Ethernet is a little bit cheaper
Personal computer	$2,500 purchase price plus maintenance, plus user support
Server machine	Depends on capacity desired. Can range from $4,000 for an Intel PC to $100K+ for a high end risk server or a minicomputer
Network cards	$150 to $600 per machine
Server accessories	$50 for each extra Megabyte of memory. $400 for each additional 200 Megabytes of storage
Laser printer	$1,000 +

In addition to the initial purchase price, it is prudent to plan on a 20% to 25% annual hardware maintenance charge. Many hardware vendors have learned to survive on razor thin hardware margins by increasingly turning to maintenance agreements for profits.

Include a hardware maintenance cost

Software

The cost of software in many cases can exceed the cost of hardware. The reason is that many types of software are needed to support the entire system life cycle. In fact, in order to support a client/server application, you have to "recreate" the equivalent of a mainframe data center! This expense can run into tens of thousands of dollars.

Many types of software are needed

If your application is the first client/server system in the company, it can be especially difficult to justify it, because all of the new tools are likely to be charged to the project.

Let's now examine the software expense in some detail. I have broken all software into three categories: the operating system and related software, the support tools, and the application development tools.

Operating system	$50 for DOS, to $300+ for a more advanced operating system like UNIX, NT, or OS/2
Network operating system	$250 for a simple peer-to-peer LAN like Windows for Workgroups, to many thousands of dollars for advanced NOS like Netware or LAN Manager
Database engine	$200–$300 for a personal DBMS like Paradox or DBASE, to many thousands of dollars for a high server DBMS like Sybase, Oracle, or Ingress
Communication packages for asynchronous communication or 3270 emulation	$100 to $400

Operating Systems

All client and server machines need an operating system. Depending on the type of server and client, the cost of the operating system can range from under $100 per user to thousands of dollars for minicomputer servers. In addition to the operating system, some type of network operating system, like Netware, Banyan, or LAN Manager, is needed for basic file, printer, and application sharing services on the network.

A network operating system can cost anywhere from $75 per node to as much as $300–$400. The variance is attributed to the size and complexity of the project. For example, it would take little effort to integrate a solution for a five-person accounting office. A very simple Ethernet network could be put in without in-wall wiring. A simple peer-to-peer NOS such as Lantastic would be more than adequate to address the needs of these users.

Complexity drives the cost

On the other hand, a large-scale application that is used by five hundred users at multiple sites is an entirely different undertaking.

Large systems cost more

Support Tools

In order to effectively support a distributed application, a number of systems management tools are necessary. This category includes software distribution tools like IBM's Netview/DM. Netview/DM can perform unattended installations, software refreshes and other configuration management functions. The table below lists the associated costs.

Support and management tools

Software distribution	$200 to $300 per node
Remote control	$50 to $100 per node
Backup and recovery	$300 to $500
Problem and change management database	Varies
Network analyzers	$7,000 to $15,000
Performance monitors	$200 to $300 per node

If your users are located at a distance, some sort of remote control tool like Symantec's pcAnywhere can help you control the keyboard of a remote machine. Using such a tool, you will be able to see on your screen everything that the user is seeing.

Remote control tool

Protocol analyzer

In a large corporate network which consists of many physical locations with multiple protocols, there is a good chance that you will need a network analyzer. A network analyzer can help you decode network traffic in order to find network-related problems.

Performance monitors and problem determination tools

Performance-related problems are some of the most difficult types of problems to solve in client/server systems. The difficulty is largely caused by the number of components that make up a networked application. To resolve a performance problem, you need a tool that can spot changes in performance and isolate the source. Unlike a mainframe environment, such tools (namely, performance monitors) are still in their infancy. Nevertheless, any assistance that such a tool can offer is better than no tool at all.

Development Tools

Development tools cost varies with system complexity

The cost of and the need for development tools varies widely. Here again, the proverbial "it depends" must be given. For a small automation project, as stated above, you might not need any development tools at all. Any application integration can be accomplished with the tools supplied with many end user applications. If, for example, you wanted to integrate a MS Excel spreadsheet with a Word document, your task could be accomplished easily through Excel's macro language and Word's WordBasic. On the other hand, if you are undertaking a large scale application development, you will surely need a language compiler, and possibly other development tools, such as 4GLs and screen-scrapers. The table below lists development tools costs.

Language compiler (C, C++, Smalltalk, FORTRAN, Basic, Pascal)	$200 to $600
Debuggers	$150 to $200
4GL languages	$700 to $7,000
Source code management library	$100 to $300 per node
Automated testing tools	$300 to $50,000

The need for software to test the newly developed systems is often overlooked. In the GUI environment, such tools provide the keystroke and mouse record and playback functions, the screen compare function, and many other useful functions. Again, the cost for these tools can vary widely from several hundred dollars per node to thousands of dollars.

Software testing tools

Purchased software, much like hardware, has a maintenance cost associated with it. Many software vendors have decided to recover support expenses through maintenance agreements. As with hardware, annual fees of 15% to 25% of the initial purchase price are common.

Software maintenance costs

How Can Client/Server Systems Cost More?

The microprocessor revolution has changed the relationship of hardware, software, and labor expenses. In many projects, the cost of software development by far surpasses the hardware costs. For this reason, a decision to develop any home-grown software must be clearly justified. If you can find a commercial package that satisfies the bulk of your requirements, it will most likely cost you less to purchase it.

More and more, software development costs can exceed the costs of hardware

Labor expenses in a networked systems development project come primarily from four areas: software development, testing, operational support, and end user training. Many cost/benefit analyses fall short in representing the true costs of labor.

High labor content is responsible for high costs

Developing networked systems requires a broad and deep knowledge of various technologies such as networking, relational databases, new programming languages, operating systems, and GUIs. The education process needed to make your programming team productive in these technologies requires time and significant expense.

Many new skills are needed

A typical "accelerated" course in just one of these technologies can last a week and cost between $1500 and $2500 per student. The cost of educating employees also includes their salaries, benefits, unemployment insurance, and travel expenses. As you can see, the cost of training can be substantial even for a very small development team.

Education is expensive

Many difficult decisions must be made	A project manager in charge of delivering a client/server system faces many difficult decisions: "Do I retrain the staff that I already have?" "Do I hire new employees?" "Should I bring in a consultant?" There are no simple answers.

The Cost of Testing

Testing distributed systems is complex and expensive	Another substantial cost of developing distributed systems, which is often overlooked, is that of testing. Distributed applications are more difficult to test than are traditional terminal-based systems. The number of components in a networked application and their interactions on the network are some of the reasons.
The GUI contributes to testing complexity	A GUI is another reason. The GUI gives users many choices for navigating a system, thus increasing the number of permutations of user actions that need to be tested.

When calculating the cost of testing one must include:

- Additional hardware needed

- Automated testing tools

- Salaries of testers and users

The Cost of Operational, Ongoing Support

Support costs of distributed systems are underrated	The most underrated expense in implementing networked applications is the cost of supporting them. This fact is especially surprising for individuals coming from mainframe environments, who sometimes fail to realize that many system maintenance activities that were done centrally in the mainframe system and taken for granted, such as data backup and recovery, are now done by the end users or their support staff.
A distributed systems support group must be created	A mini data center-like infrastructure must be created and left in place by every project, unless a company creates a central distributed systems support group. Creating these groups is both time consuming and expensive. A cost/benefit analysis should adequately reflect the true cost of this effort, which includes developing operational proce-

dures for change management, problem management, and other coordination tasks.

The support cost is ongoing, and is closely tied to the size and complexity of the system. Obviously, the cost of supporting a small departmental system with all of its users located at a single site is much lower than the cost of supporting hundreds of users in many locations.

Support costs grow with the size and complexity of a project

Figure 3.1 Typical client/ server project expense curve

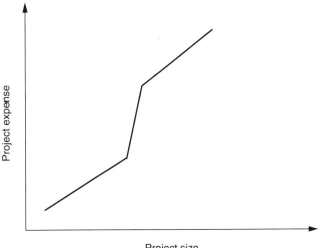

Project expense

Project size

Another factor influencing support costs is whether the LAN infrastructure already exists. If a LAN administrator is already supporting other applications, the incremental cost needed to support a new application is not as great. The most expensive project is the first application, because it creates not only the application but also the support infrastructures around it.

Subsequent projects can leverage the infrastructure created by initial projects

As the graph in Figure 3.1 indicates, support costs are fairly reasonable for a small scale project, and increase rapidly as the size and complexity of the project grows. Such expense comes from additional management tools needed for operational support. Once a large number of networked applications is deployed, an economy of scale can be achieved, and these expenses continue to grow at a more reasonable rate.

The expense curve reflects project complexity

State of Support Tools

There is a lack of good tools for distributed systems support

The best assessment of the support tools available at the time of writing this book would be "poor to nonexistent." Much software installation, problem determination, change management, performance monitoring, and administration is done via the *sneakernet*. (The sneakernet is a "technical term" for putting on your sneakers and running around between hundreds of machines with a bunch of diskettes in your hand.)

High labor content = high cost

I hope you are asking yourself questions like, "How will I install the software on 500 machines?" "How will I distribute the fixes?" "How will I configure 500 machines?" The labor cost of networked systems support can easily become the most expensive part of the project.

The ratio of system administrators to users is unacceptable

Today, it is not unusual to find a 20:1 or 30:1 ratio of users to system administrators supporting a networked system. Needless to say, this ratio must be improved to bring distributed systems costs to a more affordable level.

Developing rules and procedures requires time and significant expense

Additional support costs can be attributed to the development of support rules and procedures. Since this technology encompasses so many other disciplines, existing support organizations are ill-suited to provide distributed systems support.

Distributed support requires the cooperation of technical specialists

In many shops, the support organizations are aligned by their technical specialties. For example, there might exist a database support group, a communications group, a hardware support group, and so on. These groups rarely have had to interact with each other in the past. In the distributed world, interaction between these groups is absolutely crucial (Figure 3.2).

Business Benefits

The benefits are there!

While the overall cost of distributed systems is high, when applied to the "right" problems, distributed systems can deliver tremendous benefits to the business.

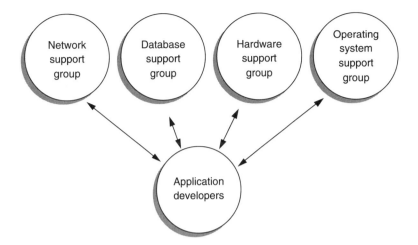

Figure 3.2 All infrastructure support groups must work closely with application developers

For many years businesses have placed a lot of emphasis on operations systems. For example, insurance companies created policy administration systems, banks created customer account information systems, and so on. Very little emphasis has been placed on what to do with the data residing in operational systems.

The initial focus of business automation has always been on operations systems

The advent of client/server computing has changed the situation, by placing more emphasis on the use of data in decision making. If you think about it from a business perspective, it makes a lot of sense to utilize the data that have been collected in operations systems for many years towards better decision making.

Client/server computing leverages existing data for decision support systems

The use of client/server technology for decision making not only improves the quality of everyday decisions, but also allows a business to plan its future strategy. For example, a trend analysis of a set of products in a retail business can reveal the market direction and expose market niches that have not been addressed.

Improved decision support systems can give a competitive advantage

Another benefit of client/server systems is the focus on the user. For many years, people have optimized computer systems for machines, not the human beings that use them. This made a lot of sense, because the cost of computer hardware far exceeded the cost of human labor. The advent of personal computers has changed all that. Just the opposite is true now. Client/server computing places the user and the user's needs first (Figure 3.3).

Client/server computing focuses on the user

Figure 3.3   Layers of client/ server computing

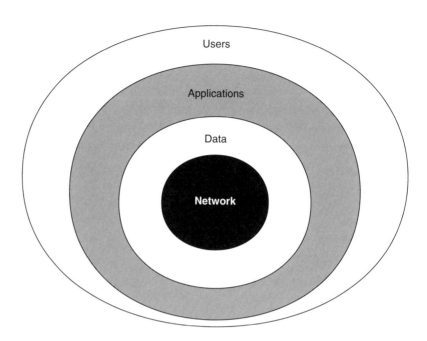

Client/server computing has made accessing data significantly easier

In the past, we subjected users to incredible journeys in search of data. We gave them answers like, "the data are located on another system, you have to get an extract form there first," or "the data on this system are in a different format. You must convert this format to my system's format." Sound familiar? The age of client/server computing brought an end to that kind of thinking. Why should a user know or care what system contains the data? He or she should be able to access them regardless of their location, format, the time of day, or the system in which the user currently happens to be.

Local area networks enabled data sharing

Such data interchange has become possible partially due to the local area network. Since all computing resources are connected to it, the network serves as the integration medium between various systems, allowing them to exchange their data.

Operating systems' data interchange facilities have also improved

Additionally, many advances in the operating systems simplified this data interchange between applications running on the same machine. Many GUI systems have built-in ways for applications to easily exchange such data. Microsoft Windows, for example, provides at least three ways to share data.

A clipboard is a Windows name for a section of memory that can be used to share information. An application can *copy* its information to the clipboard in a variety of formats. Another application can *paste,* or transfer this information to itself.

MS Windows offers a clipboard for applica-tion-to-application data exchange

Another powerful way to exchange data in a Windows environment is through the use of Dynamic Data Exchange (DDE, Figure 3.4). DDE is a client/server protocol for exchanging data and commands between Windows applications. This exchange can take place in real time, on demand. One application takes on the role of client and requests information, while another becomes a server and supplies the client with the information requested.

Dynamic Data Exchange is another powerful integration tool

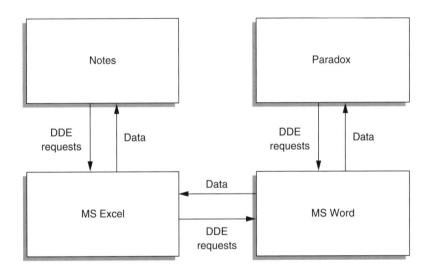

Figure 3.4   Applications exchanging data using DDE

Graphical User Interface

The cornerstone piece of client/server applications is the GUI. Time and time again, when used correctly, the GUI has proven itself easier to use than text based systems. The use of graphics to represent busi-ness objects makes it easier for users to learn how to use a system and better understand its facilities.

The GUI offers more ways to present data

A big benefit of GUIs is that they foster a common look and feel to all applications. A home-grown application can look and feel like applications purchased from software vendors. The common look and

The GUI offers applica-tion interface consistency

feel allows users to quickly learn new applications, which results in substantial savings to the business in terms of training expenditures. Another benefit is that the users *like* using them, and that translates to higher user productivity and improved job satisfaction.

Justifying Client/Server

Example of a client/server advantage

For many companies, client/server computing has created new opportunities to stream-line their business processes and gain a real competitive advantage. For example, consider an insurance company that sells its products through a network of agents. In the past, an agent would have to visit a prospective customer, gather all necessary information, and mail that information to the home office, where the underwriting staff would get involved before a quote was issued. The whole process took close to four weeks. This means that potential clients had about four weeks to shop around and buy a competitor's product.

Client/server systems can drastically improve many business processes

After a client/server system was put in, a salesperson was able to collect all of the necessary information at a customer's site, by entering it into his or her laptop PC. As soon as that information was entered, it was transmitted back to the office for immediate approval and a quote. In 80% of the cases, an agent was able to present a customer with a proposal in a matter of minutes and close the deal!

Business reengineering should be done in conjunction with client/server implementation

This example demonstrates that client/server system implementation and business reengineering are inseparable. A rethinking of how the business is done must occur before a new system is built. Client/server computing makes it possible to improve the newly redesigned business processes.

The business benefits of client/server computing outweigh the additional cost

While the IS costs are likely to increase, a client/server system can lower the overall business costs. Too often, the business focus is only on the cost of IS—its staff, hardware, software and so on. A much broader perspective is needed. Take the previous example, where a sales process was streamlined. If the focus had rested solely on the cost of IS, the bigger picture would have been lost—the cost to the business in lost revenue! That cost is certainly far more important.

Quantifying the cost of lost business opportunities is much more challenging than identifying salaries and system expenditures. It takes a keen understanding of the business and what really matters to the clients.

Lost business opportunities must be quantified

To help you further understand the benefits of a client/server system, I have created this simple checklist. Instead of focusing on what the system should provide, I have chosen to emphasize the kinds of things it should avoid. A well-designed client/server application should *not*:

A client/server system should not...

- Require users to reenter data from one application to another, or from one screen to another

- Require users to worry about how to convert data from one format to another

- Involve systems people for producing reports

- Prevent users from accessing data from any application, or any screen

- Require users to go through extensive training to be able to use the system

- Be unavailable to the users for an extended period of time

Examples

In order to demonstrate the cost-benefit analysis let's try to apply it to two hypothetical, but very realistic proposals. We will call the proposals *A* and *B*.

Example A

Example *A* involves a law office having about 20 lawyers and a 5-person administrative support staff. Currently, they use a minicomputer from Wang, mostly for word processing. The office is leasing the Wang system for $20,000 a month. A list of their user requirements appears below.

A small law office

- Reduce overall system expenditure

- Provide the ability to share documents

- Provide easy-to-use word processing

- Provide the ability to print a large volume of documents quickly

- Provide a library of standard template letters that can easily be modified

- Provide a basic customer billing system that is accessible from any workstation

A simple peer-to-peer LAN

One possible solution would be to replace the Wang system with an Ethernet network of 25 personal computers. Since the lawyers and their administrative assistants occasionally need to share documents and the high-speed printer, they will need a simple peer-to-peer network operating system like Lantastic. Such a network is a good solution for this office, because it is easy to administer, does not require a dedicated server machine, and offers adequate performance.

Off-the-shelf word processing

A standard package will satisfy the word processing requirement. Since most of the users are already familiar with Windows, we will pick MS Word for Windows. To satisfy the template requirement, we will customize Word with a series of template documents that the users can choose from when they create a document. The built-in language of the word processor, WordBasic, can help us there.

A database package

The company has chosen to outsource template and billing system development to a local specialist. To create a billing system, we will use an end user database package such as Paradox and store the database on a shared drive.

The cost/benefit analysis for this proposal might look as follows:

Hardware (25 PCs @ $2,100 ea.)	$52,500
Operating Systems	incl. with PCs
Communications software (peer LAN)	$600
Development cost	$4,000
Development software	incl. with wp.
Training users (1 day Windows + app)	$3,750
Training developers	$0
Training operational staff	$600
DBMS	$250
Professional services	$4,000
Developing support procedures	$50
Operational support, employee cost per year	$10,000
Operational support, tools	$0
Annual hardware maintenance	$10,500
Annual software maintenance	$970
Testing, tools	$0
Testing, employee cost	$0
Total initial outlay	$76,720
Ongoing annual cost	$21,470

Lease savings over the next 5 years (initial outlay * maintenance) – the cost of leasing at $20,000/month	$1,041,400
Increased employee productivity, measured as time reductions to produce documents (25 employees @ 4,000 per year) over 5 years	$500,000
Total savings over 5 years	$1,541,400

Example *B*

A car rental agency

A large car rental company wants to replace their existing MVS CICS with an easy-to-use client/server application. This application would be used by rental agents located throughout the United States. The approximate number of users is 800. The current system has the following problems:

- It is very difficult to use. The training period for an average user is 2 to 3 weeks. This situation is unacceptable, because the turnover rate at this rental company is very high.

- The management does not have up-to-date information on car rentals by region. Without this information, it is hard to put together promotional campaigns to increase business in those regions.

- The amount of data entry that the rental agent has to do is overwhelming. This not only creates poor morale, but also results in long customer lines.

Therefore, the users want to see a system that has the following characteristics:

- It should be easy to use. The training period should be reduced to 1 or 2 days.

- It should collect, display, and summarize information for the upper management to use in strategic planning.

- It should eliminate redundant data entry in order to lighten the workload and improve customer satisfaction. The company also wants to handle the yearly increase in business without hiring more employees.

Leveraging a GUI

The solution involves developing a graphical front end to the current system. Such a front end will make use of easy-to-understand graphical symbols and actions. The chosen platform for this front end is Microsoft Windows.

Improved decision support

In order to gather daily operational information, the new system will make use of a local database (one per office). A report application will be run at the end of the day, which will summarize daily data and send it to the company's central database.

To eliminate redundant entry, the company has decided to make use of portable bar code readers, allowing rental agents to quickly identify and retrieve contract information.

Bar coding…

Here is a cost/benefit analysis for the proposed system.

Costs

PC hardware (800 PC @ $1,500 each)	$1,200,000
Portable bar code readers	$240,000
Operating systems (client incl.) server	$450
Communications software (3270 emul.)	$12,000
Deployment cost (2 employees for a year + travel)	$130,000
Development software (a 3270 font-end tool plus a C compiler)	$5,000
System development cost (2 programmers for 8 mo.)	$100,000
User training (800 users * $300 per user)	$240,000
Training developers	$3,000
Training operational staff (4 @ $1,000 each)	$4,000
Client/server DBMS (one for each office)	$90,000
Professional services (4 weeks of consulting)	$12,800
Developing support procedures	$1,500
Operational support, employee cost	$190,000
Operational support, tools (a remote control package and a software distribution system)	$90,000
Annual hardware maintenance	$190,000
Annual software maintenance	$21,490
Testing, tools	$50,000
Testing, employee cost	$40,000
Total initial outlay	$2,408,750
Ongoing annual cost	$ 401,490

Benefits

Increased employee productivity (expected increase of 5% computed as salary savings —ongoing)	$ 800,000
Reduction in total business expenses (computed based on hirings that need not take place—ongoing)	$400,000
Improved decision making via acces to data (the company believes that this can increase sales by 2% over the next 5 years)	$10,000,000
More user-friendly applications, resulting in a decrease in the turnover of 5% of 18,000 employees (the cost to the business is about $6,000 per employee	$5,400,000

Conclusion

Any significant project expenditure must be justified

Cost justifying networked applications is a difficult, but necessary task. A bad decision, especially on a large scale implementation, could have a serious impact on the bottom line. Therefore, a cost/benefit analysis must be a prerequisite to any systems expenditure.

Chapter 4 addresses another difficult but very important task—vendor management. The goal of that chapter is to provide you with suggestions on how to find and leverage providers of distributed systems technology.

Suggested Reading

"Justifying Client/Server," Gartner Group briefing, June 28, 1993. Gartner Group can be reached at (203) 967-6700 voice, or (203) 967-6191 fax.

J. Fred Weston and Eugene F. Brigham, *Essentials of Managerial Finance,* New York: Dryden Press, 1985.

4

Vendor Management

One of the most important decisions a project manager has to make is the choice of technology supplier. This process goes beyond finding a tool that seems to address your current requirements. A technology supplier is an important partner and can either make or break your project. Being a partner means sharing in the success of your undertaking, as well as suffering the consequences of its failure. This chapter examines this often complex, but absolutely critical, issue.

The tone of this chapter should not be interpreted as being vendor hostile. There are many vendors who consistently meet and often surpass their customers' expectations. My objective is to make the reader more aware of how to make a relationship with a vendor mutually beneficial.

Vendor Selection

First and foremost, the vendor's product must at least meet the majority of your business requirements. The basic question that must be answered is: "Can the current release of the product meet our needs?" If the answer is "no," you can either look for another product or decide on the merits of those requirements that cannot be met. If the product does not meet many important requirements, it is time to look at another product. As obvious as it sounds, it is often surprising to see many otherwise competent project managers fall into a vendor's "promised land" that goes something like this: "we currently don't support these features, but we plan to very shortly."

Determine how closely the product meets your business requirements.

Not only should the product meet your current requirements, but the overall long term direction of the vendor should be in line with your company's direction (Figure 4.1). For example, if a vendor is more attuned to Microsoft's long term strategy and architecture, and your company has been and plans to stay a predominantly IBM shop,

Determine your vendor's alliances

chances are that long-term disagreements might arise with this vendor's product direction and priorities.

Figure 4.1 Industry alliances

Microsoft camp

IBM camp

UNIX Camp

DEC camp

Understand your vendor's business

It is important to understand that all vendors are driven primarily by the needs of their existing customer base and long-term objectives. Therefore, a project manager must learn as much as possible about the vendor in order to set realistic expectations. Some of the fundamental questions that need to be answered are:

- What is the largest revenue source for the vendor?

- How committed is this vendor to the product that you will use?

- What percentage of their revenue does this product represent?

- What is the company's financial situation?

- Who are the largest shareholders of the company?

- What are the long term goals of this company?

- Who are the major customers, and how are they using the product?

- How long has the product been in production?

Be cautious of beta products

If your company is oriented toward short-term results, be cautious about using beta products. The danger is in committing yourself to a product that might not deliver on its promises. I have witnessed too

CHAPTER 4   VENDOR MANAGEMENT

many situations where the only party that really benefited from a beta program was the vendor. Unless you really believe that the product will make a huge contribution to your project, it is unproductive to spend your valuable time helping a vendor track down problems in its product.

There is an incredible amount of vendor *hype*. Often the promises are grandiose, but the delivery is sorely lacking. To avoid unpleasant surprises, you should ask the vendor:

Look before you leap

- How long has the product been on the market and in use? You can't rely on the product's version number to give you that information. Often, many vendors purposely increase the version number to make you think that the product is more mature than it really is.

- Ask for several references, and understand how long they have used the product and exactly how they have used it. Ask them if they have used the product in production. Will you use the product for a similar task on the same operating system?

There are many companies that might not necessarily have set up adequate support organizations for their product. If you are planning on having many users call for support, you might simply exceed the vendor's capacity to provide adequate product support. In order to understand a vendor's support capability, ask them how many people are manning their support lines and to describe their qualifications.

Determine support structure

From a vendor's perspective, product support is one of the most expensive items on their income statements. Many vendors, especially those in software commodity markets where the profit margins are under constant pressure (e.g., spreadsheets), are no longer willing to swallow the cost of product support. They have been increasingly passing this cost on to their users. Given this situation, a project manager must thoroughly understand what type of product support he or she will receive, how much it will cost, and how the vendor recovers this cost.

Understand how the support cost is being recovered

Writing a Vendor Contract

Create a vendor contract with your important vendors

Not all vendors are equally important to your project. Some can easily be replaced at very little cost, while others can become indispensable. A project manager should prioritize all vendors in terms of their importance to the project. For those vendors that are considered your strategic partners, having a vendor contract is a very good idea.

Figure 4.2 Vendor contracts must clearly state expectations

This contract should clearly spell out mutual expectations

A vendor contract should specify in clear, unambiguous language what your expectations are of that vendor and what the vendor's expectations are of you (Figure 4.2). It must define a set of rules and deliverables that both parties will promise to abide by and fulfill. The scope of such a contract should be based not only on the existing situation, but also should take into account the entire duration of such a relationship.

Be clear

What do you write into such a contract? First and foremost, you must have a clear idea about what your expectations are of the vendor. You must be very specific. Naturally, vendors cannot read your mind. Once you know what your expectations are, write them into the contract.

Such contracts must be fair to both parties

It is also a good idea to make sure that there is some form of incentive for both parties to live up to this agreement. For example, if a vendor does not deliver on its promises, they should agree to pay some form of a penalty. Conversely, if you have promised to purchase a specified amount of a product and somewhere down the road find that such quantity is not really needed, it would be unfair not to compensate the vendor, who likely has incurred many unnecessary expenses on your behalf. This is a list of items that are typically put into such agreements:

- Products used

- Services offered

- Contract duration

- Support requirements and expectations

- Penalty for noncompliance

- Rewards for exceeding expectations

- Contract termination procedures for both parties

- Procedures for dispute settlement

The bottom line of any agreement is that it must be based on the *win–win* principle, so that both parties are motivated to live up to the agreement.

Win–win

Conclusion

Finding and choosing the "right" vendor is absolutely critical to successful system delivery. You should research every potential vendor to ensure that they share your business philosophy and will continue to provide solutions compatible with your technical architecture. The following is a vendor-management checklist that you should consider:

Vendor selection process is very important

1 Does their current product meet your needs?

2 Is the vendor's company philosophy compatible to your company?

3 Do their short- and long-term directions match where your company wants to go?

4 Do they have a positive reputation in the industry?

5 Is the vendor a financially stable company?

6 Can the vendor demonstrate applications in production environments similar to yours?

7 Have you tested the vendor's support organization? If so, have they met your service expectations?

8 Is the vendor receptive to having a performance contract with your company?

9 Can you really work with these people?

Suggested Reading

Landry, *The Software Developers and Marketers Legal Companion*, Reading: Addison-Wesley, 1993.

5

Assembling the Right Team

Client/server technology encompasses many areas of computer technology, such as communications, database management, GUIs, and so on. Therefore, it should come as no surprise that to successfully build client/server applications requires a team with a diverse technical background. In this chapter, we will explore the types of skills needed on such a team and how to make the team very productive.

First, let's examine the typical job descriptions and responsibilities for members of a client/server team.

A Technical Architect

First and foremost, every project needs a technical architect. A technical architect needs to have a broad level of knowledge in communications, operating systems, GUIs, and tools used in development. While this individual does not need to know all of the low-level, how-to details of these technologies, he or she must know enough detail to be able to intelligently reason about what is possible and what is not. Such knowledge comes from experience. Therefore, an ideal technical architect should have hands-on programming experience in many areas of computing.

A technical architect must have a broad and deep knowledge in many technologies

Another very important requirement for a technical architect is to be a *big-picture* person. He or she must visualize all the pieces that make up the application, understand their interfaces, and most importantly, must know how all the pieces fit together to produce a technically sound system. Since building client/server applications requires specialization, programmers tend to focus solely on their own components. The danger here is that unless someone understands how all of these components fit together, the system will have unpredictable behavior and will appear inconsistent to the users. In the

He or she must insure architectural consistency

worst case possible, it will not work, requiring a significant retrofitting effort.

A system architect must either possess the business knowledge or work with someone who does

A simple fact of life is that a technically sound system might not necessarily address business needs. It may be able to deliver wonderful response time to its users, but if it does not provide functionality that users need, it is of little value. In order to ensure that the system is both functionally and technically sound, an architect must either be knowledgeable in the business domain or work with someone who is. More often than not, it is difficult to find individuals that have both the technical depth and the specific knowledge of the business. Therefore, many projects have a technical architect as well as a business architect.

A GUI Designer and Programmer

The job of a GUI designer/programmer is very important

Another very important job role in a client/server development is that of the GUI designer and programmer. It is one of several factors that will determine how well the system will be received by its users. The user interface is the only component of a system that every user comes into contact with, and therefore, users will judge the system based on how well the interface helps them perform their jobs.

It is hard to find someone with the skill to build good interfaces

In some respects, the knowledge of how to build good user interfaces is still very scarce. The best way to proceed is to hire someone who has already done it on other projects. There is simply no substitute for experience when it comes to designing user interfaces. An ideal candidate for this position needs to posses these skills:

- Experience designing GUI interfaces

- Some background in usability factors

- Knowledge of the business

- Good programming skills

- Ability to work with people

In order to design effective user interfaces, a GUI designer needs to reasonably well understand the business. He or she should be very familiar with various job descriptions and their functions. Furthermore, this individual needs to know what the users of the system do every day. Only then can a system be designed to work the way users expect it to work.

A GUI designer must understand what the users do every day and how they will use the system

On one projects I was involved in, a GUI designer struggled to understand why users wouldn't want to mouse their way to a menu bar, select one item, and subsequently select another. It took a countless number of meetings to make the designer understand that users needed to perform this series of operations about 7,000 times a day and really needed to have this function made accessible by a key or a push button!

A GUI designer should also be a good application programmer. Having in-depth systems-level programming knowledge is less important. By systems-level programming I mean the ability to program on the operating system level or at the communications level. The reason is that a GUI designer's primary focus is on making the system easy to use for the programmer. A GUI designer must optimize the system for a user and does not necessarily have to worry about the system-level issues.

Systems programming skills for this individual are less important

Sometimes it is not possible to find an individual who has good user interface design skills as well as solid programming experience. In such circumstances, many companies end up either contracting with a user interface/human factors consultant or bringing in another member of the team whose job involves working on the user interface design with programmers and subsequently conducting usability studies during a system test.

A GUI designer does not have to be a programmer

Personal productivity software like word processors, spreadsheets, and databases coupled with a GUI have created another breed of programmers known as the desktop programmers. Unlike traditional programmers that code in languages like C, COBOL or FORTRAN, desktop programmers have grown up with macro languages, dynamic data exchange, and OLE. They tend to be much more oriented toward user needs and are skilled in the art of *glueware,* which involves integrating and customizing off-the-shelf software to fit the

Desktop programmers can be a source of good GUI designer candidates

needs of the users. Many of these individuals are very good candidates for GUI designer/programmer positions.

A GUI designer must be able to work well with people

Finally, a good GUI designer must be able to work effectively with many people. This job involves almost constant interaction with users and other team members. Therefore for this position, effective communications skills are just as important as technical skills.

A Server Programmer

A server programmer must be well versed in systems programming

In addition to GUI designers and programmers, just about every client/server project (unless it is absolute trivial) also needs one or more server programmers. Server programmers code application servers. Such application servers can be applications written in languages like C or COBOL, or can be stored procedures. In contrast to the GUI programmer, a server coder needs to be much more systems oriented and more technical, because a server application must be efficiently designed and coded to deliver a consistently high level of response time to its users.

Server programmers are more traditional programmers

Server programmers tend to be more traditional. They tend to code in 3GLs such as C or COBOL, have a good understanding of relational databases and SQL, and a good understanding of the operating system facilities available to them. A server programmer should also be knowledgeable in computer networks in order to be able to make intelligent decisions and tradeoffs in the physical design of a system.

A server programmer must be more sensitive to concurrency issues

The best candidates for server programmers seem to come from more system-oriented projects. For example, a programmer that has coded an I/O module used by many different applications throughout a company has already designed a widely shared system component. That would put him or her in a position to better understand how similarly multishared application servers need to be designed.

The most technical person on the project should be the server programmer

The job of a system programmer is to create the most efficient code possible. This area requires the highest level of technical proficiency. If you have a technical whiz on the project, turn him or her into a server programmer. If you don't have anyone with such abilities, I would highly recommend that you find someone.

Systems Administrator

At least one individual needs to be identified as a systems administrator. A system administrator plays several major roles. First, he or she must decide the roll-out strategy for the software. Should the software be installed on all machines at once or only on some?

Another important challenge that must be addressed is how the software will be installed on users' machines. Often, a systems administrator must create an installation routine. He or she must also decide how the bug fixes will get distributed. Will there be an automated software distribution tool or a manual diskette sneakernet distribution? A systems administrator must also plan for disaster recovery. How will the software be backed up? At what intervals? What is the exposure due to data loss or prolonged system outage? How long does it take to restore the system? A good systems administrator must be able to answer all such questions.

The job of a systems administrator is a challenging one. It requires both good technical aptitude and a good understanding of the business and how the system can impact it. He or she must be technically proficient, because the systems administrator is often the first line of support and problem determination. The more technically competent the systems administrator is, the higher the chance that any problem can get resolved in a timely manner. A good set of monitoring and problem determination tools can certainly make the job of a systems administrator easier, but it is no substitute for solid technical knowledge.

The ability to deal with people, especially under pressure, is another important requirement for a systems administrator. In fact, as much as 80% of the administrator's time is spent answering users' questions and giving them directions and advice.

Putting it All Together

Just as important as the technical skills of every individual, the team members must be able to work together. Building a client/server application requires effective teamwork and constant communications.

Since a client/server application is a conglomeration of so many different technologies, it takes a significant amount of effort to bring all of them together into a coherent and consistent system.

Client/server team ingredients

In addition to the technical skills already mentioned, there are certain personality characteristics that make some programmers more suitable to client/server development. They are:

- Willingness to build, scrap, and build again, with no fear of trying

- Willingness to constantly learn new things

- Self-motivation

- Ability to work with incomplete and ever-changing specifications

- Ability to function with very little direction

- Insatiable desire and passion to make the project work

Experimentation is inevitable

One of the most difficult concepts to get used to, especially for programmers coming from a mainframe background, is that it is perfectly okay to experiment a little. The fact of the matter is that when building client/server applications that consist of many different technologies, it is difficult to accurately predict what the performance might be, or even if the entire system can function. Unlike the mainframe world, where just about every application is built with the same tool, in the heterogeneous client/server world predictability is hard to come by. Therefore, a little bit of experimentation is perfectly acceptable. I am certainly not advocating a "build first and design later approach." Many obvious recoding situations can and should be prevented, once some experience is gained. However, one of the most effective ways to gain such experience is by experimenting.

Continuous learning is a must

As the client/server world continues to evolve, continuous learning is a necessity and a way of life. If someone is not comfortable with continuous learning, he or she should remain on legacy systems maintenance. In the course of a project, you might find yourself changing or adding development tools, databases, networks, etc., which requires learning new concepts. Some people are natural learners. Given a book and a new product, they can educate themselves in a very short amount of time. Needless to say, these are the people that you want to have on your team.

Above all, building client/server applications requires real commitment from everybody involved. Long hours, emergencies, and tight dead lines are a way of life. Every member of the team must have a passion to see the project succeed.

Commitment, commitment, commitment

This chapter concludes our discussion of business and management issues. In the next chapter, we will focus on the technology of distributed systems.

Suggested Reading

Tom DeMarco and Timothy Lister, *Peopleware,* New York: Dorset House Publishing, 1992.

Edward Yourdon, *Decline and Fall of the American Programmer,* Yourdon Press, Englewood Cliffs: Prentice Hall, 1992.

6

Computer Networking

APPC, TCP/IP, 4GLs, network routers, hubs…you've just about had
it! What do all of these acronyms stand for? What is their importance? How do you put it all together? One of the hardest things for
someone starting out in distributed computing is getting oriented to
the technology and its terminology. Starting a client/server project is
like dropping a person off in the middle of a deep forest without a
map or a compass—this analogy holds nine times out of ten!

The goal of this section is to help you get oriented in the "woods" of
distributed computing. By its end, you should have a good understanding of the technology that makes up distributed systems.
Perhaps more importantly, you will be better able to make logical,
rational decisions on how distributed computing can be applied to
your business needs.

The Local Area Network (LAN)

We shall begin by studying local area networks, because they serve as
the foundation of distributed computing technology. The LAN is the
means by which communication takes place among the many components of a distributed system.

LANs are at the heart of distributed computing

As is the case with many other computer terms, *local area network* is
not entirely accurate and has many different meanings. Some people
use *LAN* to refer to the physical wiring used. For example, you will
hear someone say, "We have a token ring LAN." Other people use
LAN to refer to the network operating system they use, such as Novell's NetWare or Microsoft's LAN Manager.

The term "LAN" is used inconsistently

In the strictest sense, the term *LAN* refers to the physical wiring and
the transmission technology. Ethernet, token ring, and FDDI are some
of the most popular types of LANs in existence today (Figure 6.1).

LAN refers to a physical network

Figure 6.1   Popular LANs

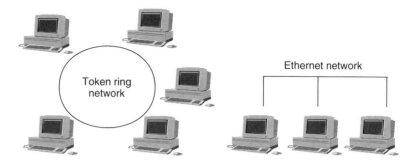

LANs used to be local

As their name implies, local area networks were originally intended to remain local. *Local* in this case means a network that connects devices in the same building or around a campus. LANs were distinct from metropolitan area networks (MANs) and wide area networks (WANs). Similar to other new inventions, the application of LAN technology has been extended way beyond its original intent.

Today, LANs can span continents

Today, LANs are no longer limited to a set of buildings. Combined with the ever increasing power of personal computers and faster network speeds, the business community has turned LANs into corporate communication highways which can connect user sites around the world (Figure 6.2).

Figure 6.2   Interconnected LANs spanning continents

A closer look at networking will yeild a computer communications model

In order to understand how LANs work, we first must learn how computers communicate with each other and how such communications software is written. Computer networking is the foundation upon which all client/server systems are built. We will explain networking

CHAPTER 6   NETWORKS

using a communications model which will give us a framework for understanding computer communications. We will then quickly substantiate our theoretical knowledge with examples of how the concepts are implemented in today's products.

The Open Systems Interconnect (OSI) Model

The OSI model of computer communication was developed by the International Standards Organization to ensure that all computer communications software was written in a consistent way, with the ultimate goal of allowing all computers—regardless of size, function, or make—to communicate in a consistent way. Without such a standard, computer communication on a wide scale would not be possible.

The OSI model defines a standard for how computers should communicate

For example, in the early 1960s, IBM alone had hundreds of different communications protocols. It didn't take very long for IBM to realize that to achieve computer networking on a large scale, a consistent approach had to be devised. Thus in 1974, IBM came out with its networking blueprint, the Systems Network Architecture (SNA).

IBM recognized the need for communications consistency, and created SNA

In this chapter, we will use the OSI model to demonstrate how computers communicate in a structured manner. The OSI model of networking has yet to achieve universal acceptance. Nevertheless, it can serve as a useful reference for explaining how computer communication takes place.

The OSI model is a good framework for learning computer communications

Communications software is written using a software layering approach, where each layer performs a given function (Figure 6.3). Each layer uses an adjacent layer to perform functions it can't do on its own. When data must be sent to another computer, they are passed down through the layers. The layer on top always calls the layer below, which in turn calls the layer below it, and so on, until the data are transmitted to another device, where the reverse cycle takes place.

Networking code is written using a layered approach

Figure 6.3   The OSI model

| Application |
| Presentation |
| Session |
| Transport |
| Network |
| Data Link |
| Physical |

Data are passed up and down the layers

The reverse cycle involves the lowest layer passing data and control to the layer about it, which in turn does the same until the data are finally received by the application (Figure 6.4).

Figure 6.4   Flow of data in communication layers

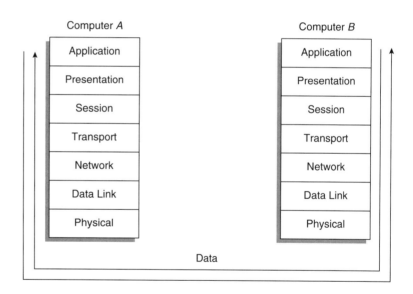

Computer *A*

| Application |
| Presentation |
| Session |
| Transport |
| Network |
| Data Link |
| Physical |

Computer *B*

| Application |
| Presentation |
| Session |
| Transport |
| Network |
| Data Link |
| Physical |

Data

Envelope analogy…

An easy way to understand communication between the network layers is to use the analogy of an envelope. Imagine that the data are passed from one computer to another in a large envelope, which contains a smaller envelope inside it, which in turn contains yet another smaller envelope inside it, and so on (Figure 6.5).

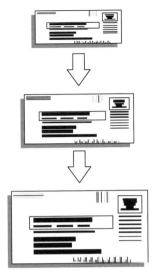
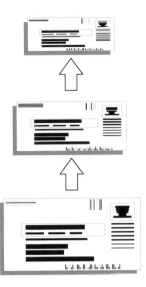

Figure 6.5   Data passing

How do these envelopes get put together? The process starts when a program running on computer *A* wants to communicate with a program running on computer *B*. The sender program calls its topmost layer. The topmost layer creates some data it wants its counterpart layer on computer *B* to read. It places its data, along with the data sent by the program, in an envelope and passes down the envelope to the layer below it (*calls* the next layer).

The data and control are sent to subsequent layers

All the layers below perform an essentially similar task; that is, they create data which they want to send to their counterpart layers on the destination machine and attach to it the data passed from the layers above.

Each layer adds its control information

Once the message (the envelope) arrives at computer *B*, the process works exactly in the reverse. The bottom layer removes its information from the envelope and passes the remainder of the data to the next layer, which removes its data and passes the remainder to the layer above. Again, this process continues until the user application has received its data.

As the data arrive at their destination, the process works in reverse

Now let's examine the function performed by each layer of the network more closely.

The Physical Layer

The physical layer is the medium of transmission

We will start with the physical layer. For any communication to take place, there must exist a physical path on which an electrical signal (data) can travel. Therefore, the function of the physical layer is to simply send the data on the wire. The most common media for data transmission is an electrical wire. It is important, from a physical layer perspective, to understand the different types of wiring available.

UTP is often the choice

Many types of wiring can be used in local area networking, but the greatest popularity seems to belong to the wiring that is already in place in many modern buildings—unshielded twisted pair (UTP). Many buildings are automatically wired with UTP in order to support the telephone system.

UTP can be voice or data grade

A word of caution about UTP is in order: UTP comes in two flavors, *voice grade* and *data grade*. Voice grade wiring has significant limitations in reliability and speed when used in the transmission of data.

High-speed LANs require data grade wiring

If you are planning to make use of the emerging 100-Mbit/second LANs, the only safe choice is to use UTP grade 5 cable. It has been successfully tested at up to 100 Mbits/second, and therefore will work with many emerging high-speed standards, such as 100BaseT, CDDI, and ATM. We will examine these networks later in the chapter.

Shielded twisted pair is another good choice

Another popular type of wiring is the shielded twisted pair (STP). The shielding protects data from electromagnetic interference (noise), allowing STP to support higher data rates than UTP. STP has also been successfully tested with many emerging high-speed networks.

Coaxial cable can also be used

There are also two types of coaxial cabling that can be used in LANs, sometimes known as the *thin* and *thick* Ethernet trunks. Coaxial cabling is similar to the cable used to connect VCRs and other video equipment. For many years, coaxial cabling has been used to connect dumb terminals to the mainframe.

Fiber optic technology is being increasingly used to connect networks

In recent years, fiber optic technology has become an increasingly popular choice, especially when used as a high-speed *bridge* connecting remote sites, or as a backbone connecting various LAN segments.

Fiber optic cable transmits data in the form of light, and is therefore free from electromagnetic interference. It also offers a significantly higher bandwidth. Of course, all that comes at a price: fiber optic cable is still very expensive.

What type of cabling should you use? Many times the choice has already been made for you, due to existing wiring. When you do have the freedom to choose, consider the price, bandwidth requirement, desired network speed, and the duration of stay at a given location.

The choice of wiring depends on your objectives

The Data Link Layer

Obviously, the wire does not transmit data by itself. Some convention must be agreed upon by all of the devices that want to send data. Such conventions are known as *data link control specifications,* and you probably know them as Ethernet, token ring, Arcnet, or FDDI.

The data link layer is responsible for the transmission of data

The data link specifications determine the type of wiring supported, the network topology (bus or ring), the partitioning of data into frames (small messages), and acknowledgments.

Data link specifications determine many physical attributes

Ethernet

Ethernet is a very popular standard. Its approach uses a carrier sense multiple access (CSMA) protocol. In plain terms, this approach is known as *send and pray.* A computer that wants to send data on the network first very briefly *listens* to see if any other device is sending data. If no other computer is sending data, it then proceeds to send its data (Figure 6.6). In a busy network, several devices may try to send data at the same time, resulting in data collisions. A collision detection mechanism detects such collisions and causes the retransmission of data.

Ethernet networks use the CSMA/CD technology

Figure 6.6 Ethernet network

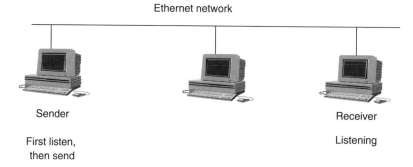

Ethernet network

Sender

Receiver

First listen,
then send

Listening

Ethernet is a popular, reasonably priced LAN for small- and medium-sized networks

It is important to understand the strengths and limitations of Ethernet. If you are building a small- or medium-sized network, Ethernet will likely meet your needs quite well. It is relatively inexpensive and easy to install. It also delivers excellent performance. A new Ethernet standard called 10BaseT (10 Mbits/second over UTP) has improved many of the original shortcomings of Ethernet. For example, Ethernet requires a *star* wiring topology, where each computer is connected by a separate cable to a hub. The hub serves as the concentrator, and also performs some management functions, such as disconnecting workstations from the rest of the network if problems develop.

Large or heavily utilized LANs require predictability

However, if you are building a very large scale LAN that will consist of tens of thousands of nodes and carry large amounts of data, you should avoid using Ethernet. Large networks with high utilization should be predicable in their behavior. One should be able to calculate precisely how the network will be impacted if additional stations are added and what the throughput of the network will be under heavy utililization. This predictability (sometimes called determinism) is difficult to achieve using the collision detection approach.

Token Ring

In a token ring network, a token must be captured before the data can be sent

Another popular LAN data link protocol is called *token ring*. In a token ring network, a token travels on the network in a circular fashion. When a device wants to send its data, it must first capture the token. Once captured, the token can be used to carry the data to a specified destination. When the data are received by the destination device, the token is released and becomes available to other devices (Figure 6.7).

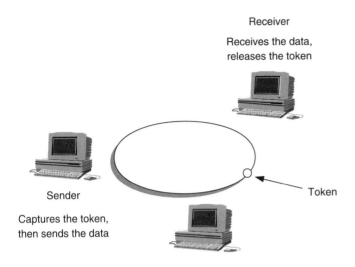

Receiver

Receives the data, releases the token

Figure 6.7 Token ring network

Sender

Captures the token, then sends the data

Token

At first glance, this solution might seem awkward. The question you are probably asking yourself is, "Will getting the token become a bottleneck?" The token travels at nearly the speed of light, so that even in a very busy network getting the token is hardly a problem.

The token travels around the ring at very high speed

Token ring networks are deterministic. Put another way, their behavior is mathematically predictable even under the heaviest of loads. Unlike Ethernet networks, their throughput is constant, regardless of the number of devices or the amount of data sent. This feature makes a token ring network a good choice for large, enterprise-wide LANs.

The behavior of a token ring network is predictable

FDDI

Fiber Distributed Data Interface (FDDI) is another popular data link control protocol for fiber optic networks. FDDI is a 100-Mbit/second network, which represents roughly a tenfold increase in speed over today's popular networks. Like token ring, FDDI uses a ring topology, with two data paths transmitting data simultaneously, in opposite directions. Some companies are trying to extend this protocol to other cabling systems in order to bring down the cost of FDDI

FDDI is a 100-Mbit/ second network which requires fiber cabling

networks. CDDI is one such example. Instead of using fiber, CDDI uses ordinary copper wire for transmission.

FDDI is the most widely used high-speed LAN, but it is still expensive

Of all emerging new standards, FDDI has been used the most to date. If you really need a 100-Mbit/second network today, FDDI is really your only choice, but be prepared to pay a premium. The biggest impediment to wide acceptance of this standard remains its cost.

100-Megabit/Second Ethernet

There are several competing high-speed Ethernet proposals

The Ethernet bid to remain a popular networking choice comes in two proposed standards that are battling each other in the standards committees. They are the IEEE 802.12 standard, called AnyLAN, and the IEEE 802.3 100BaseT standard. 802.12 has been proposed by Hewlett-Packard. It is called AnyLAN because it can accommodate both Ethernet and token ring formats. Thus, this emerging standard offers a convergence path for all popular networks.

It is not clear today which proposal will dominate

The proposed 802.3 standard is really an extension of today's popular Ethernet standard, 10BaseT. 100BaseT would continue to use the CSMA/CD media access method. Which one of these emerging standards is likely to dominate remains to be seen.

The Network Layer

The network layer helps devices on the network find each other

So far, we have discussed physical wiring and various schemes for regulating the transmission of data, but we have not addressed the problem of how devices find each other on the network. After all, a network could consist of thousands of machines, connected by bridges and routers. The function of the network layer is to figure out how to traverse an arbitrarily complex network—to put it simply, how to find a path between any two devices that want to communicate. In technical terms, these functions are called *addressing* and *routing*.

Another important function of the network layer is to provide *media independence,* which means that sending data should work the same way regardless of the network type, e.g., token ring, Ethernet, X.25, etc.

Example: Internet Protocol (IP)

To make this discussion more concrete, let's briefly discuss how the network layer works in one of the largest networks in the world—the Internet. The Internet protocol (IP) is responsible for providing network layer functions on the Internet. Specifically it provides three functions:

- Global addressing

- Data delivery service independent of media type

- A routing strategy for transferring data through a very large network

In order to connect to Internet, you first must be assigned a unique address. This address has nothing to with the built-in addresses in your network adapter. The Internet address is a 32-bit number that consists of three parts:

- A network identifier

- A host (a *computer,* in Internet lingo) identifier

- A subnet identifier derived from the host identifier

A typical Internet address might look something like this:

192.70.95.95

where each number is represented by a byte.

Your next logical question might be, "How does this Internet address get mapped into a real address on my network adapter? After all, that is the only address that can be used to send data to my computer." There are several ways that address mapping can take place. One approach algorithmically maps an Internet address to a physical address and vice versa. For this approach to work, there must exist a one-to-one mapping of addresses.

Another mapping approach is protocol based

Another approach is to *discover* the physical address via a protocol. Imagine a server that keeps a table which consists of two columns. One column contains Internet addresses, the other contains physical addresses. When a host needs to know a physical address, it simply sends a message to the server. If the physical address is not present, the server discovers it and stores it in its cache for subsequent requests.

Datagram service is the foundation on which other functions are built

Now let's examine how the Internet's data delivery service works. The delivery service provides only a *datagram* capability. A datagram is a short message (usually less than 1024 bytes) that can be sent to any address on the network. Datagrams are not guaranteed to be delivered. The upper layers must provide that service. The only type of data integrity that is done at this layer is a checksum algorithm.

Routing determines where the datagrams are forwarded

The next logical question is, "How does the Internet protocol figure out how to deliver a datagram from one machine to another?" This is accomplished by the Internet's routing (Figure 6.8). First, a comparison is done between the source machine's network segment address and the destination machine's network address. If they are identical, the datagram is sent directly to the destination machine.

Figure 6.8 Internet routing

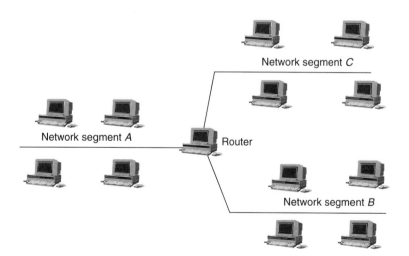

Network segment C

Network segment A

Router

Network segment B

Routers connect network segments

If the network segment addresses are not the same, the datagram is sent to the router. Routers connect multiple network segments. The function of the router is to figure out on which network segment to send the datagram. The routing process continues until the datagram is received by its intended destination. A natural question might be, "How does the router know about other network segments?" The router dynamically learns of other network segments through interactions with them. Naturally, some initial information about other network segments must be loaded from disk.

To recap, the functions of the network layer are:

- A rudimentary data delivery service between any two nodes

- A logical (hardware-independent) addressing scheme

- Routing of packets

The Transport Layer

The transport layer is the first layer at which there is a direct connection between the sender of data and the receiver. This is not to be confused with a similar function provided by the network layer. At the network layer, the scope of communication involves intermediate nodes. In contrast, the function of the transport layer is to provide end-to-end connectivity, where all of the intermediate nodes involved in communication are transparent.

Transport protocols provided end-to-end connectivity

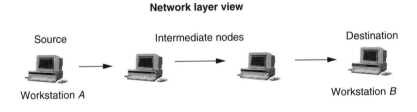

Figure 6.9 Network layer view versus transport layer view

The transport layer provides transparent communication	In Figure 6.9, above, workstations *A* and *B* are communicating. Basically, the network layer knows how to get from one point (workstation) in the network to another. In contrast, the complexities of the network, i.e., all the intermediate nodes, are hidden at the transport layer. As far as the transport layer is concerned, there is a single *connection* between workstation *A* and workstation *B*.
Message decomposition/ composition is controlled by the transport protocol	Another important function performed by the transport layer is the decomposition and reassembly of user messages. Let's say your application wants to send a 15-Kbyte message. Since the entire message cannot travel on the network intact, it needs to be broken down into smaller chunks. Each chunk is then sent to the receiver, where the recomposition of the massage takes place. The transport layer is responsible for ensuring that the chunks of a message are put together in the same order as they were sent.
Transport protocols are the first real network programming interfaces	The transport layer is the first real programming interface provided to programmers. Many client/server systems, such as network operating systems, client/server DBMSs, and groupware products are built using these interfaces. Why are all these products written to comply to transport protocols? Because they offer physical media independence; that is, a program written for TCP/IP sockets, NetBIOS, or IPX does not have to be changed at all when its moved from an Ethernet environment to a token ring network. Some of the most popular transport protocols are TCP/IP, IPX/SPX, NetBIOS, and IBM's APPC. We will briefly review them here.

TCP/IP

TCP/IP has been a proven and reliable solution for many years	Transmission Control Protocol/Internet Protocol (TCP/IP) is one of the most mature and widely used transport protocols in computer communication. In existence for over twenty years, TCP/IP has extensively been used in government, educational, and commercial settings. It is a very robust protocol, because it was initially designed to run on slow, error-prone WANs.
TCP/IP is truly open	TCP/IP is the only protocol in the industry that does not belong to a vendor. Thus, it is truly an open protocol, and can be obtained from public domain sources or commercial products. The *vendor neutrality*

of TCP/IP has helped establish it as the de facto standard in communications interoperability in a multivendor environment.

TCP/IP is a lot more than a transport protocol. It terms of the OSI model, it spans from the network layer all the way up to the session, presentation, and application layers (Figure 6.10).

The TCP/IP stack spans many OSI layers

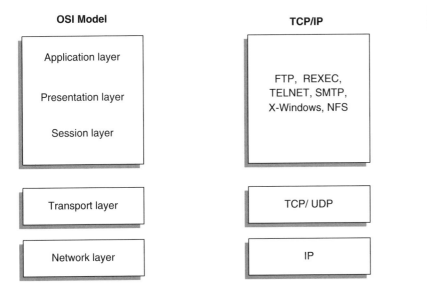

Figure 6.10   TCP/IP layering

The use of TCP/IP is certainly on the rise. This is due to several trends taking placing in the industry. The first is the explosion in the use of the Internet network. TCP/IP is the foundation on which the Internet is based. The second reason is the popularity of client/server applications and the UNIX operating system. Many database management systems, such as Sybase and Ingress, originally were written to run on UNIX. Since many client/server applications require a high-end DBMS, they often require a UNIX server, which in turn, brings in TCP/IP.

TCP/IP's popularity is on the rise

IPX/SPX

IPX/SPX protocol is the foundation on which Novell's network operating system is built, and therefore runs in most Netware shops. IPX/SPX is based on Xerox PARC's XNS protocol. While IPX/SPX is

IPX/SPX is the foundation for Netware

often perceived to be a PC-based protocol, its many implementations are now available for UNIX, NT, OS/2, and UnixWare.

A bindery is used to advertise available resources

One of the most popular features of IPX/SPX is its ability to use the Netware *bindery.* A bindery is a place where applications can advertise services available to other applications. When an application wants to find out about what kind of id resources are available on the network, for instance, it makes a call into the bindery.

NetBIOS

NetBIOS was conceived as an extension to PC BIOS for accessing networks

In the early 1980s, IBM contracted with another firm to create a standard application interface for networking, just as PC BIOS (basic input/output system) served as a common application interface to the PC hardware controls. The idea was to define a standard API that would remain the same regardless of transmission technology (data link control), so that an application would not have to be changed when moved from a PC network to a token ring network.

NetBIOS enjoys wide support...

This feature quickly earned NetBIOS popularity, and it became the de facto standard interface in PC networking. Even today, many non-NetBIOS environments, such as NetWare, offer NetBIOS emulation.

...however, the long term prognosis for NetBIOS looks bleak

In the last several years, the popularity of NetBIOS has been diminishing, for several reasons. NetBIOS is simply an application programming interface and does not map well into the OSI communication model. A fundamental problem is that it is not routable. NetBIOS was designed for small networks of personal computers, and unlike TCP/IP, it does not break the network down into a collection of network segments. Instead, NetBIOS treats the whole network as one logical segment. This shortcoming and the increasing popularity of UNIX and TCP/IP are continuing to squeeze NetBIOS out of the marketplace.

APPC

APPC is IBM's peer-to-peer protocol

Advanced Program-to-Program communication (APPC) is IBM's SNA protocol for writing distributed transaction-oriented applications. It has been widely used to provide distributed transaction processing in the mainframe environment. For example, CICS inter-systems communications uses APPC to enable CICS applications running on a variety of mainframes to exchange information.

APPC is an extremely robust protocol. This makes it a good choice for distributed transaction processing, where recoverability of data and transactions, as well their coordination, are very important.

Over the last several years, as personal computers and workstations have became more and more powerful, APPC has become increasingly available in these environments. As you have probably guessed, the "robustness" of APPC is not without a price. APPC takes a significant amount of memory to run, and there is more overhead involved in session establishment than with some other protocols.

Now that we have examined these four popular transport protocols, let's look at some of the other features they offer. Most transport protocols provide two types of services: *connection-oriented* service and *connectionless* service.

Connectionless service, also known as a datagram service, gives programmers the ability to send and receive data to any node in the network or to broadcast data to all nodes or to a group of nodes. The programmer has only to supply the destination address. As its name implies, a sender of data does need to establish a connection with its destination.

The advantage of connectionless communication is its speed. There is very little overhead involved in sending a datagram on the network. Of course, there is a price to pay. The downside of connectionless service is twofold:

- The maximum size of the message is limited (usually less than 512 bytes)

- The delivery of the message sent is not guaranteed! It is the programmer's responsibility to ensure that the message actually gets to its destination.

Example: NetBIOS Datagrams

NetBIOS supports data-gram service

As an example, let's briefly consider how the NetBIOS transport protocol provides connectionless service. NetBIOS uses the term *datagram* to refer to its connectionless service. A datagram can be sent from any machine to any other machine or to a group of machines, provided the programmer specifies:

- The destination address, which is a NetBIOS name, e.g., *John*

- Where the message is stored

- Data length (the default maximum datagram size is 512 bytes)

- The name number, which is returned from the ADD_NAME function (NetBIOS initialization routine)

This sample function shows how a NetBIOS datagram gets sent:

```
short SendDatagram(char *name,          /* destination name */
                   void *message,       /* pointer to message */
                   short size,          /* how long is it */
                   short name_num       /* name number */
                   )
{
    struct SREGS sregs;              /* DOS register structures */
    union REGS regs;
    NCB ncb;                            /* network control block. */
                        /* need to communicate with NetBIOS */

    memset( &ncb, 0, sizeof(NCB);      /* clear out NCB */

    /* fill in the network control block */
    ncb.NCB_COMMAND = SEND_DATAGRAM;
    ncb.NCB_NUM = name_num;
    ncb.NCB_BUFFER_PTR = (void far *) message;
    ncb.NCB_LENGTH = size;
    strcpy(ncb.NCB_CALLNAME, name);

    /*set up register pointers to ncb */
    sregs.es = FP_SEG((void far *) &ncb);
    regs.x.bx = FP_OFF((voif far *) &ncb);

    /* send the datagram */
    int86x(0x5C, &refs, &regs, &sregs);
}
```

Connection-Oriented Service

In contrast, a connection-oriented service offers guaranteed message delivery. The transport protocol takes care of retransmitting the data in case of data corruption. Another benefit to connection-oriented service is that the size of the message can be reasonably high. For example, using NetBIOS a maximum message size could be up to 128 Kbytes (CHAIN.SEND). Connection-oriented service is often provided via *sessions*.

Connection-oriented service requires session establishment

A session (also called a *connection* or a *virtual circuit*) is analogous to two people having a phone conversation. Once one person dials another, and that individual answers the phone, a session is established. Both individuals can speak and listen for a response. In the same way, when two applications are in session, both can send and receive data. Another way to visualize a session is to imagine a pipe between two applications (Figure 6.11).

A session is analogous to a telephone call

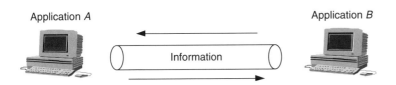

Application *A*

Application *B*

Information

Figure 6.11   A session between two applications

A session is explicitly terminated when one of the applications decides to disconnect. A session can be of two types: *full duplex* and *half duplex*. In a full-duplex session, both parties can send and receive data simultaneously. In contrast, in a half-duplex session only one party can send data at a time. The majority of network protocols today offer full duplex connection-oriented service, with the SNA APPC protocol being a notable exception.

Sessions can be full or half duplex

Example: SPX Sessions

To give you a better understanding of how connection-oriented services work at a programming level, we will examine the Sequenced Packet Exchange (SPX) protocol. This protocol, along with the Internetwork Packet Exchange (IPX) protocol, is the foundation on which Novell's network operating system, NetWare, is built.

SPX is the Netware session protocol

**Figure 6.12   A typical SPX
exchange**

```
SPXInitialize()                              SPXInitialize()

                                             SPXListenForConnection()
SPXEstablishConnection()

                    Session established

                                             SPXListenForSequencedPacket()
SPXSendSequencedPacket()

SPXTerminateConnection()
```

*SPX must first be
initialized*

The first command issued by an SPX application is the initialization
call to the SPX subsystem (Figure 6.12). This call determines whether
SPX is installed on the system where the application is running:

```
SPXIntialize(BYTE *majorRevisionNumber,
             BYTE *minorRevisionNumber,
             WORD *maxConnections,
             WORD *availableConnections);
```

*SPXInitialize returns
some system capacity
information*

After the call returns, `majorRevisionNumber` and `minorRevision-
Number` contain the version number of SPX installed on this machine.
`maxConnections` is the maximum number of sessions that the
machine has been configured for, and `availableConnection` contains the number of session that can be used by the application.

Once initialized, a client SPX application establishes a session with a
server by calling

```
SPXEstablishConnection(BYTE retryCount,
                       BYTE watchDog,
                       WORD *connectionID,
                       ECB *eventControlBlock) ;
```

Most of the parameters are self explanatory, but some deserve comment. In SPX, a *watchdog* process monitors the health of the session.
The watchdog monitors session activity. If the session fails, the watchdog records that event in the completion code of the *ECB* field.

*Applications communi-
cate with SPX using
ECBs*

What is ECB? An event control block (ECB) is a data structure that
contains variables used to maintain the state of communication. It is a
required parameter for many IPX/SPX functions. Similar to Net-
BIOS's Network Control Block (NCB), ECB is *filled in* with

CHAPTER 6   NETWORKS

appropriate data before the call is made to SPX. An ECB is also used to return information to the application.

The `SPXEstablishConnection()` call also returns a connection identifier, which uniquely identifies a particular session to SPX on subsequent calls. The life span of a connection identifier is the life span of the session. Once a session is terminated, the connection id is no longer valid.

A connection identifier is a session handle

So far, we have addressed the client (requester) side of SPX. We will now examine what happens on the server side. Before a session is established, a server application must be in a ready state to accept it. This is accomplished with:

A server process must be listening for incoming connections

```
SPXListenForConnection(BYTE retryCount,
                       BYTE watchDog,
                       ECB  *eventControlBlock );
```

Once a session is established, both applications can send and receive messages until one of the applications terminates the connection, with

```
SPXTerminateConnection(WORD ConnectionIDNumber,
                       ECB  *event control block );
```

The Session Layer

The session layer in the OSI model is responsible for providing additional services, above the raw data sending and receiving services of a transport layer. One example of such service is user security validation. When a session is established, a userid and password are sent to the session partner for validation. If validated, a session becomes fully established; otherwise, it is disconnected.

The session layer builds on the transport layer to provide services like security

Other common functions performed by the session layer are synchronization, checkpointing, and crash recovery. Synchronization and checkpointing are often necessary in transaction-oriented programs. In transaction processing, a TP program performs a series of actions known as a *logical unit of work* (LUW). An LUW might involve changes to a database, a file, or both. An LUW represents one atomic transaction. Either all of the changes done are committed and kept, or none are committed and the entire transaction needs to be rolled back.

Other session layer services include synchronization, check-pointing, and crash recovery

APPC is a good example of transaction synchronization service

The best example is the transaction synchronization service in IBM's LU6.2/APPC protocol. When two applications (known as transaction programs) are in session using APPC, they can agree to the degree of coordination that both will follow. For example, they can agree to define a set of *syncpoints*. A syncpoint indicates that a program has reached a certain state.

Synchpointing example

A simple example might look something like Figure 6.13. Program *A* sends several messages to program *B*. Because it wants to make sure that program *B* gets to the predefined point before proceeding, program *A* issues a syncpoint request. Only after program *B* issues its syncpoint response, will the two transaction programs continue to communicate. In a more elaborate example, if one of these programs fails, its session partner could cause the program to roll back any changes made in the current unit of work.

Figure 6.13 APPC synchpoints between two applications

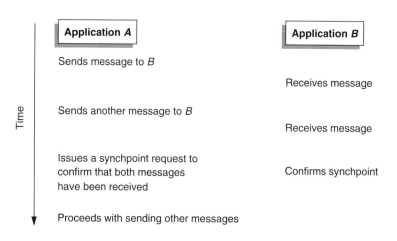

The Presentation Layer

The role of the upper two layers is less certain

While most providers of network products agree on the first five layers of the OSI model, very little agreement exists on what the remaining two layers should do. In general, the function of the presentation layer encompasses:

- The compression of data for efficient transmission on the network

- Data conversions, like ASCII to EBCDIC, big-endian–little-endian, etc.

- Other useful services that are frequently performed by many applications

The Application Layer

The application layer consists of the applications that use the network. Client/server databases, communications gateways, and network operating systems are all examples of applications that take advantage of the network. We will examine these applications in more detail in subsequent chapters.

The application layer is provided by network enabling systems

Figure 6.14 displays the OSI model and products and standards that map into its layers. This chart is certainly not all inclusive. It merely tries to relate the products and buzzwords that you probably already know to this network computing model.

The table of products and their relation to OSI

Application	Sybase, Oracle, Lotus Notes, Netware, LAN Manager, etc.
Presentation	Data compression and translation products
Session	APPC, FTP, telnet
Transport	TCP/UDP Sockets, NetBIOS, IPX/SPX, APPC
Network	Internet Protocol, APPN, XNS IDP, IPX
Data Link	Token ring, FDDI, Ethernet, X.25
Physical	Coaxial, fiber, shielded and unshielded twisted pair

Figure 6.14   OSI layers and how some products map into them

When you are confronted with a new network acronym or a product, try to map it into the OSI model based on the function that it provides. This simple activity will put the product or a buzzword into perspective, and will help you to understand the big picture, so that you can make informed decisions.

You should be able to map any new product to an OSI layer

Suggested Reading

Andrew S. Tanenbaum, *Computer Networks,* Englewood Cliffs: Prentice Hall, 1981.

Barry Nance, *Network Programming in C,* Carmel, IN: QUE, 1990.

Transmission Control Protocol/Internet Protocol Programmer's Reference, IBM publication SC31-6077. IBM publications can be ordered from IBM Corporation, Information Development, Department 245, Rochester, MN 55901.

Data Communications Concepts, IBM publication GC21-5169-6. IBM publications can be ordered from IBM Corporation, Information Development, Department 245, Rochester, MN 55901.

Alex Berson, *APPC Introduction to LU 6.2,* New York: McGraw Hill, 1990.

Local Area Network Technical Reference, IBM publication SC30-3383-03. IBM publications can be ordered from IBM Corporation, Information Development, Department 245, Rochester, MN 55901.

Schnaidt, *Enterprise-Wide Networking,* Carmel, IN: SAMS Publishing, 1992.

William H. Roetzheim, *A C Progremmer's Guide to the IBM Token Ring,* Englewood Cliffs: Prentice Hall, 1991.

IBM NetBIOS Application Development Guide, IBM publication S68X-2270. IBM publications can be ordered from IBM Corporation, Information Development, Department 245, Rochester, MN 55901.

Gerald D. Cole, *Computer Networking for Systems Programmers,* New York: Wiley, 1990.

"Network Protocols for Database Developers," *DBMS Magazine,* January 1994.

7

Operating Systems and Network Operating Systems

The evolution of operating systems has been going on for many decades. Much of the progress in the operating system world, as well as other computing disciplines, was made by observing an existing operating system and improving upon it. For example, UNIX has its roots in Multics, MS-DOS has borrowed some features from UNIX and CP/M, and VMS has many features of RSX. When you closely examine modern operating systems, you begin to see that they are very similar to each other (Figure 7.1).

Operating systems have borrowed many features from each other

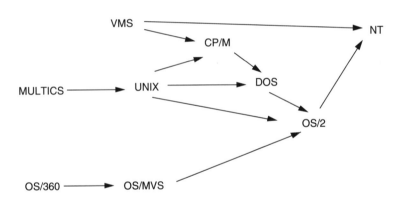

Figure 7.1 Operating systems evolution

Every modern operating system performs very similar services. It manages secondary storage devices, memory, and the distribution of CPU cycles, schedules processes, and controls the user interface, network access, and so on.

Many modern operating systems perform similar services

This leads to the natural conclusion that as long as the operating system meets the needs of your project and is well suited to client/server computing, the choice of a particular system is largely a commodity decision. Find a vendor of a popular operating system with staying power, good customer support, and obtain a commitment of support

Choosing an operating system is largely a commodity decision

from the application developer. If you apply these criteria, you can't really make a bad decision.

An ideal operating system for client/server applications should provide:

- Multiprotocol networking support

- Preemptive, priority-based multitasking

- Threads

- Support for a large number of open files, file locking, and memory mapped files

- Interprocess communication

- Virtual memory management

- Robustness

- Security

Networking

An operating system should be able to support multiple transport protocols simultaneously

Well-designed support for network communications is certainly a requirement. An operating system should be able to effectively support a number of transport protocols, in many cases simultaneously. For example, operating systems such as UNIX, OS/2, VMS, and NT are well suited for this task.

Support for TCP/IP, NetBIOS, and IPX/SPX is essential. This area is a serious limitation of MS-DOS.

At the very minimum, an operating system should support TCP/IP, IPX/SPX, and NetBIOS. If these three protocols are not supported, the operating system will not be able to integrate into today's client/server environment (Figure 7.2).

Network support in MS-DOS is weak

The lack of available memory below the 1-Mbyte line and the lack of multitasking are the primary reasons behind MS-DOS's limited network capability. While many ingenious workarounds have been implemented, network support in MS-DOS remains weak.

CHAPTER 7 OPERATING SYSTEMS

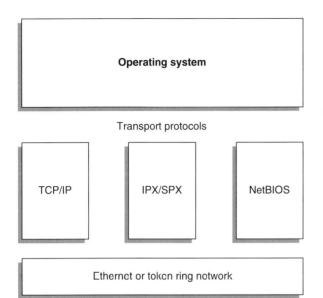

Figure 7.2 Operating systems supporting multiple protocols

Preemptive Multitasking

Another important requirement is preemptive, priority-based multitasking. In preemptive multitasking, the operating system controls the distribution of CPU cycles among the running tasks. A task is roughly equivalent to a running program. A processor can be taken away from one task and given to another if the second task has a higher priority.

In a preemptive system, the operating system controls access to CPU

Preemption is important because it guarantees fairness and consistency of CPU access for all the tasks. It prevents a single task from "hogging" the CPU. In a client/server environment, that is important, because a server must be able to deliver a uniform and predictable performance on every transaction, under any condition, to all users. An important and time critical task must get priority over other tasks.

This orderly distribution of CPU cycles assures fair access for all applications

An important benefit of preemptive multitasking in a client/server environment has to do with background processing. For example, as a designer of a client/server application you might want to retrieve the next screenful of data from a DBMS in the background, while the user is looking at the first screen. Obviously, you want to perform this

Preemptive multitasking allows smooth background processing

task without affecting the user. This is where priority-based preemption can help. By setting the background data retrieving task to a lower priority, the system will continue to be responsive to the user, even while the database task is retrieving the data in the background.

MS Windows lacks preemption

If you have tried to do any background processing in the current version of MS-Windows, you have probably observed that multitasking in Windows can take place only if all the running applications in the system are willing to cooperate.

Support for Multiprocessing and Threads

Threads belong to processes

A process or task roughly is equivalent to a running program (although a program could be made up of many processes). Processes, in turn, are made up of threads. Threads are the lowest (atomic) units of execution (Figure 7.3).

Figure 7.3 Operating system supporting multi-threading

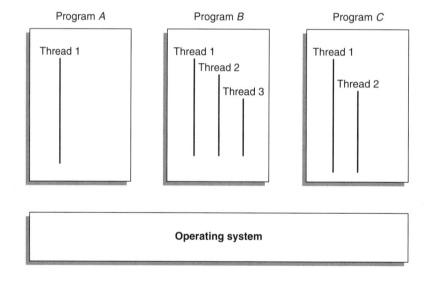

Multiuser support is thread or process based

In a client/server application, a server application must be able to handle many simultaneous requests coming from user workstations. In order to act on more than one request at a time, a server application must make use of either multiple processes or threads. This design allows every user to run independently, giving the server program the highest possible throughput and excellent response time.

Another way that operating system concurrency features might be utilized to improve the overall performance of a system is by breaking a task into a number of subtasks that could be performed in parallel. For example, you might want to design an application server that receives a request to perform some sort of a computation and return the result to a client. This could be done by using two threads (Figure 7.4). The first thread would receive client requests, place them on a queue, and immediately return to receive the next request. The second thread would take the request from the queue, perform the desired computation, and send the reply back to the client.

Threads can be used to shorten the overall time needed to perform a task

Figure 7.4   Use of threads

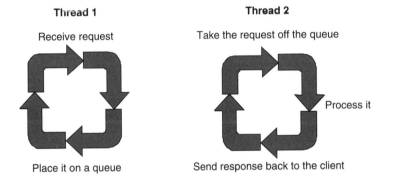

Thread 1

Receive request

Place it on a queue

Thread 2

Take the request off the queue

Process it

Send response back to the client

In this simple example, we have used two independent tasks collaboratively to perform a client's request. Threads are a good way to perform subtasks in parallel, and thus to shorten the overall time needed to perform a task. Of course, not all requests have subtasks that can be performed in parallel, but whenever they can be used, threads are a powerful tool.

Not all tasks can use multiple threads

Another way that threads can be used is to mask the difference in I/O speeds between fast and slow devices. For example, you would not want to make the user wait for his or her 50-page document to print. One way to handle this task is to create a printing thread, and to perform such printing in the background, letting the user proceed with other work.

Threads can be used to mask the difference in speeds of various I/O devices

File System Support

A server must efficiently support large files, and large numbers of
open files, because many files are accessed simultaneous from server
applications on the behalf of user requests. This is especially true in
Windows and OS/2 applications, which often consist of many
dynamic link library files. Such files get opened and closed very frequently. Naturally, an operating system supporting such applications
must process file handling as efficiently as possible.

Advanced file handling techniques such as memory mapped files can
greatly improve the performance of a server application, by minimiz-
ing physical I/O and making use of the primary memory.

Ideally, an operating system should provide built-in file recovery features that can be used to quickly reconstruct files in case of a physical
system failure. This feature is especially needed in OLTP server applications. One example of such a file system is MS Windows NT's
NTFS.

Just as important is the need for file record level locking. A database
server, for example, should be able to lock a certain range of records
in a file and prevent others from accessing it. Additionally, multiple
levels of locks are desired. If a user is simply browsing a database,
other users should be able to browse the same database simultaneously. The file locking mechanism must allow an application to
provide as much concurrent access to the file system as possible in
order to support multiple user requests that are characteristic of the
client/server environment.

Interprocess Communication Facilities

In a multitasking environment, it is common to have tens or even
hundreds of processes or threads running at the same time. These processes and threads may belong to one or more applications that need
to communicate with each other.

Such communication takes place through the interprocess communication facilities, such as semaphores, shared memory, signals, and pipes. Using semaphores, for example, one thread could signal another on the completion of some task. Figure 7.4 demonstrates this case, where the receiving thread signals the processing thread that a request is ready to be processed.

Semaphores, pipes, shared memory, and other mechanisms are used in interprocess communications

On many occasions, concurrently executing threads and processes must be able to share or exchange data. For example, a database server application often needs to cache some data in a shared memory so that they can be accessed by multiple users (i.e., multiple threads or processes).

Thread and processes must be able to exchange data

Virtual Memory Management

A server application supporting a large number of users must rely on the operating system to provide efficient and fast memory management. Most advanced operating systems implement what's known as *virtual memory* management. The term *virtual* simply means that the operating system can create the illusion that there is more memory in the system than the actual amount of physical memory in the computer.

Virtual memory can exceed the amount of physical memory

Figure 7.5   Virtual memory

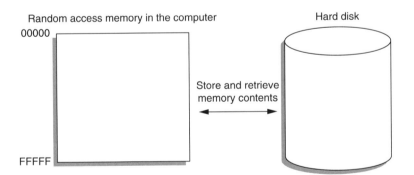

This is accomplished by using disk storage, in addition to RAM, to store memory contents (Figure 7.5). An operating system must be able to quickly and efficiently move data or code fragments (technically known as pages or segments) from disk to memory and vice versa.

Disk storage is used to store memory contents

	The benefit of a virtual memory management system to client/server
Virtual memory can support very large programs efficiently	applications is that it allows them to allocate and manage large amounts of memory. Additionally, virtual memory minimizes the amount of RAM needed to run a large application, because the entire application need not be present in memory to execute: only the code and data pages that are referenced in a program need to be in memory.

Robustness

An operating system must be fault resistant

Another important operating system requirement is robustness. This is an absolute must, especially for a server. Unfortunately, many people still think of personal computers and workstations as machines used by individuals, not realizing the implications of downtime, where one such server machine can incapacitate the work of hundreds of people! Therefore, a server operating system must be extremely robust.

Application problems should not impact the whole system

Being robust means preventing an application from bringing down the entire system. If an application encounters some form of exception, only it should be terminated. All other applications should continue to run as if nothing happened.

No Ooperating system is totally crash proof

While it is virtually impossible to build totally crash proof systems, many modern operating systems have come very close. MS Windows NT and IBM's OS/2 both offer excellent crash protection features.

Security

Client/server applications often deal with sensitive data

Security is another area that is frequently overlooked. Most client/server applications need to protect and allow access to information on a need-to-know basis. The responsibility to provide security clearly belongs in the operating system code, and not in application enabling resource managers such as DBMS, transaction processors, and application servers, as is often done today. Unfortunately, very few micro-based operating systems provide such security services, with MS-NT being a notable exception.

If security mechanisms are built into the operating system, a user would have to log on only once. Logging onto multiple applications would not be necessary, because the user's access information could be shared with many application enablers, such as DBMS or TP Monitor.

Security belongs in the operating system

Network Operating Systems

The most widely used distributed applications today are network operating systems. Network operating systems quickly became part of the underlying infrastructure on which networked applications can be developed. Many organizations are able to justify LANs on the basis of functionality provided by such systems.

Network operating systems are the best examples of distributed systems in use today

A network operating system basically extends many functions provided by the local operating system. The table below explains what functions are extended and how.

Network operating systems extend operating system functionality

Operating system	Network operating system
Local file system	Extends the local file system to be accessible by other computers in the network (file server)
Local printing	Allows other computers in the network to access a printer (printer sharing)
Local devices	Extends local devices, e.g., modems, to be accessible by other machines attached though the network

Redirection

The key concept behind all network operating systems is *redirection*. As the word implies, redirection sends requests made from the local operating system to the network operating system.

Key concept—redirection

Let's suppose we want to edit the contents of a file located on drive k: that physically belongs to the file server (Figure 7.6). We issue a

Redirection example

file open command which translates into a command to the local operating system to open and read a file. A local operating system examines the request and decides that drive k : is not a local drive. It then passes on the request to the redirector component of a network operating system. The redirector sends the request to the file server.

Figure 7.6 Network operating system redirection

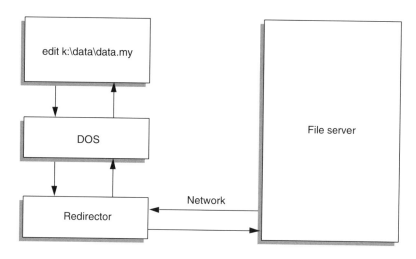

The file server performs file manipulation on behalf of the client application

The file server determines that the file resides on a file server drive, reads some data out of the file, and sends them back to the client machine, where they are returned to the editor. The editor is totally unaware of the fact the file *read* request was actually done by the file server. This concept is known as *network transparency.* The fact that the network was involved in satisfying its request was totally transparent to the editor.

Redirection can be extended to other devices

The notion of redirection is used not only in file manipulation requests, but also for requests sent to serial and parallel ports. For example, if we have a high-speed modem attached to a file server, it can be shared by many workstations. The client machines don't physically have modems attached, but their COM1 : ports are redirected to use the COM1 : port on the file server machine. Any data sent to the local COM1 : port are automatically forwarded to the server's COM1 : port. Here again, the redirection is transparent to the application.

Architecture of a Network Operating System

Network operating systems are distributed applications; that is, they consist of at least two components; a client component and a server component. A client component runs in every machine attached to the network. It allows any machine to request services like file reads and writes, printing, etc., from the server. Naturally, the function of the server is to perform such services.

A network operating system is a distributed application

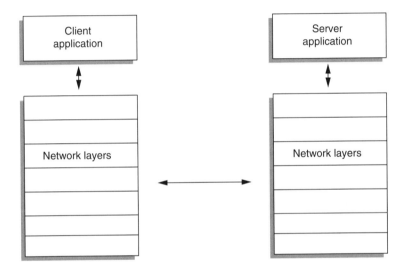

Figure 7.7 Client/server interaction

Popular Network Operating Systems

There is no shortage of network operating systems on the market today. Novell, one of the pioneers of network operating systems, still commands the largest share of the market. It is built on top of the IPX/SPX network protocol (reviewed earlier), which is based on original work done at Xerox. Novell's NetWare comes in many flavors and is widely supported by many ISVs.

Novell's Netware is still the king

Other popular network operating systems are Banyan Vines and Microsoft's LAN Manager and its derivative products, like IBM's LAN Server.

Other popular network operating systems

Peer-to-Peer Network Operating Systems

A peer-to-peer network operating system is a good alternative for smaller networks

In the last several years, a number of peer-to-peer network operating systems, like Lantastic, Windows for Workgroups, and NetWare Lite, have entered the marketplace. They are primarily designed for small workgroups (under 80 users) and are typically easier to administer than are client/server network operating systems. The term *peer-to-peer* implies that any machine in the network can be configured to be a client, a server, or both, which means that any user can make the local drive, printer, or other devices available to other users.

A peer-to-peer network operating system trades capacity for simplicity in administration

In a peer-to-peer network operating system, there is no such thing as a dedicated server. The advantage is, of course, less administration, and the disadvantage is that a nondedicated device can support only a fraction of the users possible with a dedicated device.

Example: IBM's LAN Server

IBM's LAN Server is a MS LAN Manager derivative

Continuing in the spirit of this book for presenting high-level concepts with a dose of practical detail, we will now examine how IBM's LAN Server works. LAN Server is a Microsoft LAN Manager derivative. While sharing many features of its ancestor, LAN Server has implemented many new and useful features, like the *domain*.

Domains simplify administration

A domain in a LAN Server world is roughly equivalent to a group of people working on similar tasks, independently of their geographic location. For example, a company might have a finance domain, a marketing domain, and a product development domain. The biggest benefit of the domain is that it simplifies user administration. Once a user logs onto a domain, a network administrator can automatically assign a set of network resources to him or her, such as file directories, printers, and modems. This task is especially simplified when users are assigned to groups, because network resources can be allocated at the group level.

LAN Server can run on several protocols

LAN Server can run over a number of transport protocols. The most widely used, and the system's original protocol, is NetBIOS. Now LAN Server can also run over a TCP/IP network.

There are two physical components to LAN Server: the client and the server. The client component for DOS or OS/2 needs to be physically installed on every workstation. In some environments, like banks, where security is especially important, LAN Server can support diskless workstations. In such cases, workstations are booted remotely from the file server via RIPL (remote initial program load).

LAN Server supports diskless configuration

The server component runs on OS/2. The benefit of having a server component run on a general purpose operating system like OS/2, NT, or UNIX, is that it can also be used to run other applications. In other words, the server machine does not have to be dedicated solely to the file serving needs.

The server component runs on OS/2

The core architecture of IBM's LAN Server and other MS LAN Manager products is based on a services concept. A server is actually a collection of processes working together, where each service performs a specific task. For example, an *lsclient* service needs to run in order for a user to log onto a server. Users can add their own services to LAN Server. A good example of such an add-on service is the Microsoft SQL Server product. SQL Server can be started and stopped using LAN Server commands. We will examine SQL Server in more detail later in the book.

Services make up the servers

The downside, if there is any, to IBM's LAN Server is its weak support among ISVs. While the situation has improved over the last couple of years, such support remains well behind that enjoyed by NetWare.

ISV support for LAN Server is weak

Which Network Operating System Should I Use?

Many core functions provided by network operating systems are virtually identical in all products. Given the commodity nature of this business, your decision should be made based on:

Selection factors for a network operating system

- The price of the product

- Ease of use and administration. Remember, the administrator's and users' time is money.

- Availability of applications and utilities from ISVs and a general acceptance of the product in the marketplace. This is largely determined by the market share of a product. If you heavily rely on buying versus developing your applications, make sure that applications you are planning to buy are certified to run on the network operating system of your choice.

- Ability of the product to scale as the number of users increases or decreases. For example, a large enterprise with hundreds of users will need a directory service and strong wide area network capabilities.

Suggested Reading

James L. Peterson and Abraham Silberschatz, *Operating System Concepts,* Reading: Addison Wesley, 1985.

Ted J. Biggerstaff, *Systems Software Tools,* Englewood Cliffs: Prentice Hall, 1986.

Thomas, Rogers, and Yates, *Advanaced Programmer's Guide to UNIX System V,* New York: McGraw Hill, 1986.

Stephen Coffin, *UNIX: The Complete Reference,* New York: McGraw-Hill, 1988.

H. M. Deitel and M. S. Kogan, *The Design of OS/2,* Reading: Addison Wesley, 1992.

Gordon Letwin, *Inside OS/2,* Redmond, WA: Microsoft Press, 1988.

Mitchell Marx and Penelope Davis, *MVS Power Programming,* New York: McGraw Hill, 1992.

Yukihisa Kageyama, *CICS Handbook,* New York: McGraw Hill, 1989.

Tom Sheldon, *Novell NetWare 4: The Complete Reference,* New York: McGraw Hill, 1993.

IBM OS/2 Lan Server, IBM publication 75X0968. IBM publications can be ordered from IBM Corporation, Information Development, Department 245, Rochester, MN 55901.

Microsoft LAN Manager Programmer's Reference, Redmond: Microsoft Press, 1990.

8

Database Management Systems and Application Development Tools

The power of today's workstations and server machines, coupled with increases in network speeds, has given many database vendors the opportunity to take an old concept and change it into something new. I am referring to using relational databases in a client/server setting.

Client/server databases are an extension of existing technology

Relational databases have been extensively used for well over a decade. The main idea behind relational database management systems is that all data are stored as a set of tables. Every column in a table identifies a particular field. For example, you could have an employee table which contains information about all employees in a company. This table could consist of four columns/fields: employee name, address, date of birth, and salary.

Relational databases store information in tables which contain data records

To add, remove, or modify information in tables, relational databases have more or less standardized on a language called SQL (pronounced *sequel*). SQL is a simple, but yet powerful declarative language. *Declarative* means that it specifies *which* data are to be manipulated, but not how to access them. Accessing the data is the job of the relational DBMS engine.

SQL is the data manipulation language of relational database systems

The data manipulation part of SQL consists of 4 simple verbs: insert, delete, update, and select. By using these verbs, applications and endusers can interact with a database management system. There are many excellent books that explain relational theory and SQL. In this chapter we will focus on relational databases from a client/server perspective.

SQL manipulation language consists of four verbs

In a mainframe and minicomputer environment, relational database engines and applications execute on the same physical machine, as shown in Figure 8.1. By taking advantage of the network, the database application is no longer confined to run on the same physical

An application can run on a different machine from the database engine

machine as the database engine. Thus, a database application can run on any machine in the network. When such an application issues a database manipulation request (in a form of SQL statements), it is sent through the network to the database server, where the request is performed.

Figure 8.1 Traditional DBMS versus client/server DBMS

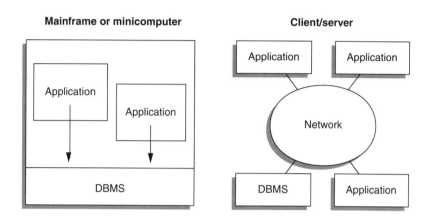

Getting applications to communicate to DBMS servers is still tricky

Sending a SQL request from a client workstation to a DBMS server requires coordination between the database software and the networking software (Figure 8.2). Both must "speak" the same transport protocols. A DBMS must also support both the client and the server operating systems. Unfortunately, this is not as simple as popping a piece of bread into a toaster.

Figure 8.2 Client/server DBMS application

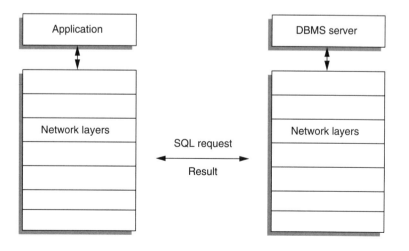

CHAPTER 8 DATABASE MANAGEMENT SYSTEMS

First, you should make sure that the DBMS you plan to use supports the operating systems at both the client (requester) and server ends. Support on the client workstation comes in the form of a library which your applications can call in order to send SQL requests to the DBMS server. Next, you should determine if the database vendor supports the type of transport protocol used in your establishment. Obviously, for communication to take place, clients and servers must be able to speak the same transport protocol, e.g., TCP/IP, IPX/SPX, or NetBIOS.

Make sure that your operating system and transport protocols are supported

After a common protocol is identified, determine if your DBMS vendor supports it. Plan on allocating a significant amount of time just to get things going. Configuration in this environment is an art of patience and persistence.

Common protocol does not necessarily guarantee communication

Database Middleware

This task of any-to-any platform connectivity can quickly become very complex. Database vendors, especially smaller ones, cannot possibly support all operating systems and all transport protocols. Furthermore, many user shops have purchased database management systems from more than one vendor, and would like to have these systems exchange data. This phenomenon has created a database middleware market (Figure 8.3). Database middleware makes it possible to connect applications to servers regardless of the transport protocol or DBMS vendor implementations used.

Any-to-any platform connectivity created the database middleware market

Figure 8.3   Database middleware

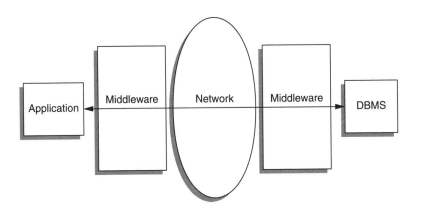

ODBC is a client-side programming interface

Over the last several years, middleware products have begun to be standardized. A standard was especially needed on the client side, because every DBMS and middleware vendor offered its own *application programming interface* (API). Imagine what a 4GL development tool vendor, like Powersoft, had to do in order to support multiple DBMS and middleware products: the vendor had to write code for each and every DBMS client API. To remedy this problem, Microsoft and the SQL Access Group have compromised on a standard client side interface for calling all DBMSs. This standard is called ODBC (Open Database Connectivity, Figure 8.4).

ODBC has top and bottom interfaces

The idea behind ODBC is simple. All user applications and end user tool providers should write to ODBC's top layer interface. The database or middleware providers should write ODBC drivers that connect ODBC applications to their DBMSs or middleware.

Figure 8.4   ODBC

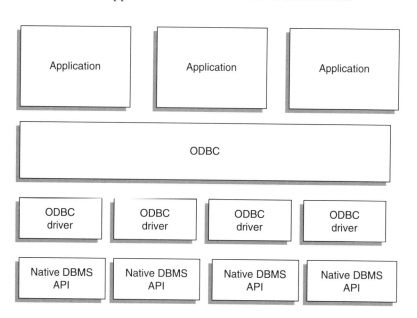

The tool vendor's job has been greatly simplified

This idea greatly simplifies the effort required to support multiple database engines. A tool vendor needs to write only to the ODBC interface, and the application should work with any DBMS that provides an ODBC driver. ODBC has now become somewhat of a de facto standard for the MS Windows platform.

Another emerging client side interface, which is championed by Borland and Novell, is IDAPI (Integrated Database Application Programming Interface). The key advantage of IDAPI over ODBC is that it can deal with more than just SQL databases. Using IDAPI, an application can retrieve data from a wide variety of data sources, such as indexed sequential storage managers (`Btrieve`), or even flat files.

In addition to SQL databases, IDAPI supports other data sources

Standardizing client interfaces is a good idea, but like any good idea it has some drawbacks. The most significant one is that such interfaces don't encourage you to take advantage of all the features found in DBMSs. If you take advantage of a particular feature found only on some database engines, the price you pay is portability. Here again, the *vanilla* approach, while very portable, tends to be the lowest common denominator.

Portability comes at a price

Database Gateways

The word *gateway* typically implies that some sort of a protocol conversion/translation is to take place. In computer networking, a gateway might, for example, convert IPX requests to APPC and vice versa. Similarly, a database gateway can take SQL requests coming in from, say, an Oracle DBMS, and translate them into a form that DB2 or other databases can understand.

Gateways link unlike DBMSs

One of the most important criteria for selecting a client/server DBMS is its ability to access other sources of data present in your shop. That often involves accessing data stored on the mainframe in VSAM, DB2, or IDMS. To address these needs, a variety of standards and products have emerged over the last couple of years.

There is a need to access data regardless of their location

One such emerging standard is IBM's DRDA (Distributed Relational Data Architecture, Figure 8.5). DRDA establishes the rules for how relational databases can seamlessly cooperate to process user requests. The concept is similar to the "rules" that network protocols must obey in order to communicate, except that these rules do not involve connectivity issues, but rather database coordination and data access issues. When the databases should commit and how, and the format in which they exchange data, are some examples of areas that DRDA defines.

DRDA wants be become the database interoperability standard

Figure 8.5 IBM's DRDA

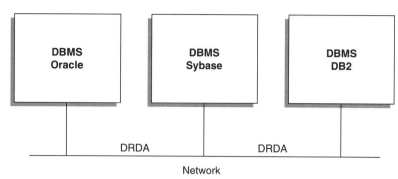

IBM's products are DRDA enabled

IBM has enabled DB2 and its other database products to support DRDA. It has also built a product called DDCS that implements DRDA architecture on the LAN. DDCS is available for DB2/6000 and DB2/2. IBM has also licensed DRDA to other database vendors in order to make DRDA a multivendor standard.

DRDA gives all database vendors an equal opportunity

One important implication here is that with an open architecture like DRDA, all vendors of database products have an equal chance at building data connectivity solutions to IBM's host databases.

Gateway Selection

Database gateways differ in functionality and purpose

Not all database gateways offer equivalent functionality. Some gateways are more suited to decision support or data warehousing projects, and emphasize flexibility over speed. Others are designed for real time access for transaction-oriented systems. It is really important to match the functionality provided by a particular gateway with your needs. Here are some typical areas of concern:

- How does the gateway deal with data types that differ between database management systems?

- Does the gateway provide both read and write, or read-only capabilities?

- Does the gateway support both static (compiled) and dynamic SQL?

- Are the data accessed in real time on demand? Is there some form of store and forward capability?

- How are security issues handled between databases?

Data Distribution Capabilities

For many departmental client/server applications, a single DBMS server is often sufficient. While some needs can be addressed with a single database server, many companies are building enterprise wide client/systems that may involve multiple database servers (Figure 8.6). The most common reason for multiple DBMS servers is to improve performance. The database servers could be located at multiple geographic sites and avoid slow wide area network links.

Enterprise-wide applications may require multiple DBMSs

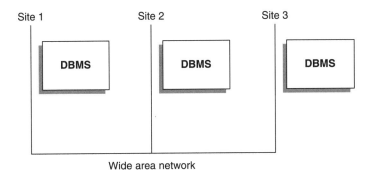

Figure 8.6   Distributed DBMS

The data can be *split* between DBMS servers in several ways. One way is to partition the data based on their geographical characteristics. For example, if your company has field offices located in various regions of the country, every field office could have a database server that contains data for that region. In this case, the database structure would remain identical for every DBMS server.

Data can be split geographically

Another way to partition the data is by a key field value. Let's say you want to keep track of everyone in the US based on their social security numbers. You can store a certain range of social security numbers on one server, another range on another server, and so on. In this example, again, the structure of the database is identical for each DBMS server.

It can also be split on a key

Finally, you can decide to distribute the database itself, by storing some tables on one DBMS server, some tables on another DBMS server, and so on. This approach is the most problematic of the three for several reasons:

- It prevents any data replication between DBMS servers because the structure is distributed, not the data.

- If table joins are performed across the network, the performance will be unacceptable. Also, most DBMS vendors do not support multiway joins to multiple databases.

- If updates of multiple tables are needed, the DBMS will have to support a two-phase commit mechanism.

Data distribution adds a lot of complexity. One obvious complexity has to do with how to keep all the data in sync in multiple databases. If a record is updated in one office, should the change be reflected someplace else? A lot depends on your application architecture, data sharing needs, and the currency of data.

There are essentially two ways to synchronize data in a multidatabase environment:

- One solution entails a real-time update of all databases involved in a given transaction. As soon as a record is updated in a local database, it must be updated immediately in other databases. This approach involves a two-phase commit, which insures that either all databases will get updated or that none will.

- Another approach replicates the data between a number of databases. This approach uses a subscribe-and-update architecture. A database can subscribe to receive changes made in another database. The changes are distributed periodically.

The first solution is typically used in a traditional OLTP environment, where transactions are short in duration and the amount of data is relatively small—for example, in the debit/credit type of transactions that are found in banking.

DBMSs differ in how they support a two-phase commit. Sybase system 4, for example, provides an API for handling a two-phase commit. It is up to the programmer to correctly synchronize the databases, which is no small effort. Oracle version 7, on the other hand, does a two-phase commit transparently to the programmer.

The second solution, data replication, is more suitable to problems that involve large amounts of data and when the data do not have to be extremely current. For example, if your application can deal with data that are a couple of hours old, replication might be a very good solution. A typical decision support application, where the data are consolidated from multiple DBMS servers for reporting, is an ideal candidate for data replication (Figure 8.7).

Data replication is a good solution for data warehousing

Some DBMSs provide replication services. Sybase system 10, for example, offers this support through the database subscription services. Any database server can subscribe to all or some of the data in another database server. Once a refresh interval is specified, all subscribers will start receiving refreshed data.

Data replication is becoming a popular feature

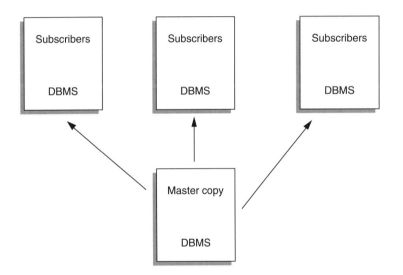

Figure 8.7 DBMS replication services

Another nice feature of the Sybase approach is that it recognizes that not all database servers are going to be up and running all the time (on-line). When a database server comes up, it will be refreshed with data that it missed while it was down.

Sybase's data replication can deal with off-line conditions

Try to avoid writing your own replication logic	If your DBMS does not provide a data replication service, you can implement it yourself. To do that, you will have to write a distributed program that consists of a data extractor on one end and a data populator on the other. The extractor reads the data from the main database at specified intervals and sends them to all interested populators. Populators run on the same computer as the DBMS and write the data to it. With major database vendors providing data replication, writing your own replication logic should be a last resort.

Application Interfaces to DBMSs

Applications interact with a DBMS using static and dynamic SQL	There are many ways that programs can interact with a DBMS. The actual mechanism largely depends on the language in which the program is written, and the DBMS language support. Basically there are two popular techniques—using static or dynamic SQL. The difference between static and dynamic SQL is similar to the difference between compiled and interpretive languages. When static SQL is used, all SQL statements are examined by the DBMS at compile time. If a program uses dynamic SQL, the SQL statements are parsed as the program executes (at run time).

Static SQL

Static SQL is favored by compiled languages	Static SQL is used by traditional 3GL languages like COBOL or C. The programmer embeds SQL statements directly in program (Figure 8.8). A DBMS provides a precompiler suited to the particular language in which the program is written. The first step in compiling a program with embedded SQL statements is to run it through this precompiler.
A precompiler translates SQL to native language calls	The precompiler accomplishes a number of tasks. The most important one is to substitute native language constructs for SQL statements embedded in the source program. For example, if the program is written in C, the precompiler will replace the embedded SQL statements with a set of C function calls to a DBMS.

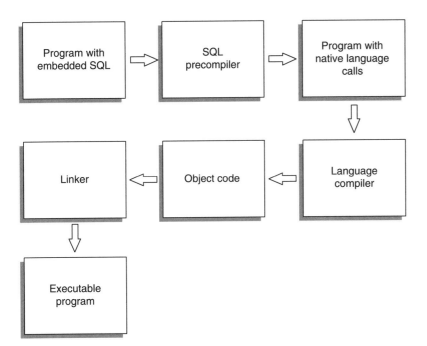

Figure 8.8 Embedded SQL
program steps

Another important task performed by the precompiler is the "compilation" of SQL statements in the program. The precompiler sends SQL statements to a DBMS, where they are first parsed for syntax correctness. If the statements are syntactically correct, the DBMS creates an access plan. As the name implies, an access plan specifies how the DBMS will go about accessing the desired data. For example, if there is a two-way join between tables, as in:

Static SQL is processed at compile time

```
SELECT *
FROM orders, products
WHERE orders.number = product.number AND
      orders.quantity <= product.quantity
```

The database engine decides the order in which conditions in the WHERE clause are performed. Additionally, a DBMS decides whether it will use an index to access the data rows or will use a linear scan (all rows).

A DBMS decides how to access the data in advance

At the end of precompilation, the SQL statement is "compiled" by the DBMS. When the program executes, the DBMS does not have to parse the SQL statement, nor does it have to decide how the data will be accessed. It simply references the particular access plan and

A DBMS does significantly less work at run time for static SQL than for dynamic SQL

retrieves the data based on instructions contained in it. This is one of the reasons why static SQL code can execute two to three times faster than equivalent dynamic SQL code.

Stored procedures use static SQL to extend programs

Another, more modern approach for taking advantage of compiled SQL is to make use of stored procedures and triggers. Stored procedures and triggers are normally written in DBMS proprietary languages that extend SQL with traditional language constructs, such as variables and loops. They can be thought of as extensions of your programs—a subroutine that your program can call to manipulate the data.

Stored procedures are another way to precompile SQL

Stored procedures, as their name implies, are compiled and stored in the DBMS. Therefore, the data access plan has already been predetermined ahead of time. Of course, this means increased efficiency for accessing data at run time.

Dynamic SQL

The advantage of dynamic SQL is flexibility

In contrast to static SQL, dynamic SQL is created by a program when it executes, at run time. A SQL statement is assembled into a string or a character array data and submitted to a DBMS for processing. Dynamic SQL, as its name implies, is more flexible than static SQL, because it can be created *on the fly,* based on user requests.

Dynamic SQL is processed in two phases

Most DBMSs require a program to submit a dynamic SQL statement in two phases. The first phase, typically known as *prepare,* checks the syntactical correctness. The second stage, known as *execution,* actually performs the required statement.

The price for flexibility is performance

The majority of 4GL development tools use the dynamic SQL interface. While the flexibility of dynamic SQL is a big plus, it should be used in applications where the SQL statement will be known only at run time. If you are writing a mission-critical, operational type of application, you should try to use static SQL whenever possible to get an acceptable level of performance.

DBMS Server Memory Requirement

How much memory does your database server need? A simple answer is—as much as you can afford. Regardless of the database engine, having more memory almost always means better performance in the database world. The reason is that the physical I/O subsystem is still the performance bottleneck in DBMS servers. The more data that can be buffered or cached in memory, the less I/Os a DBMS engine will have to perform.

Memory often equals performance

DBMS User Support Architecture

An important ingredient in DBMS performance is the internal architecture for handling multiple concurrent users. There are basically two common approaches. One way is to create a pool of processes and dedicate them to the incoming user requests. Another approach is to use threads instead of processes.

DBMS uses processes or threads

A process is roughly equivalent to a program, (even though it is possible to have multiple processes within a single program). It is a very robust mechanism. If a process encounters some form of exception and must be terminated, only a single user will be affected.

A process-based approach is more robust

This robustness is not without a price. A process takes a significant amount of memory (as much as 120 Kbytes of RAM in some operating systems). Another drawback to supporting each user on a separate process is that the *context switch* between processes is slower than threads, which means that performance of a DBMS engine would be negatively impacted. (A context switch is the time that it takes the operating system to switch from processing one process or thread to another.)

Robustness comes at a price

Threads are independent execution entities within a single process. The memory overhead is significantly less than in processes (8 Kbytes or more), and the context switch between threads is faster. The problem with threads is robustness. If a thread encounters an exception condition, the entire process, with all of its threads, is often terminated, potentially affecting many users.

Threads are faster, but less robust

Example: Microsoft's SQL Server

MS SQL Server is Microsoft's answer to a mission-critical DBMS

Microsoft became a player in the client/server database market when it licensed Sybase's DBMS technology to produce an OS/2 and a Windows NT high-end DBMS. MS SQL Server is a multiuser, high-performance DBMS designed for mission-critical work. The term *mission-critical* is often overused, so an explanation is in order. A mission-critical system requires high availability. For a DBMS, this means having such features as roll-forward recovery, on-line backups, and device mirroring.

SQL Server uses a transaction log in a roll-forward recovery

SQL Server stores all committed transactions (changes to a database) in a transaction log. In case of a system failure such as a power outage or a hard disk failure, it is likely that some committed transactions would not be reflected in a database. A roll-forward recovery is used to make sure that all committed transactions have been written to the database. This is usually done at DBMS initialization time.

SQL Server can place database objects on separate physical devices

Another high-end SQL Server feature is its support for multiple devices and segments. A device is used to store database objects such as tables, indexes, and stored procedures. To the operating system, a device is simply a file. A segment allows you to control the placement of database objects in various devices. To gain performance, you should try to place database objects across several physical drives. For example, when tables are stored on one drive and transaction logs on another, you can take advantage of the fact that disk read operations to two physical devices will take less time than performing two reads on a single disk.

Data mirroring increases data availability

SQL Server also allows you to mirror database devices. *Mirroring* means writing data simultaneously to two places instead of one. If one disk drive fails, the system can still continue to work.

SQL Server Programming

SQL Server offers client- and server-side APIs

SQL Server provides programming interfaces on the client and server sides. On the client side, all SQL Server applications are written to a DB-LIB library. Originally, this library was a call-level interface used by programs written in C. Now a client side program can be written in C, COBOL, Visual Basic, and 4GLs that either directly use DB-LIB, or get to it through an ODBC interface.

On the server side, SQL Server offers an interface called Open Data Services. Open Data Services is designed for writing server applications that can communicate with other applications or integrate multiple data sources. This is an extremely valuable tool, because it allows for the integration of existing legacy systems. An application running on a client can be totally unaware of the fact that the data it is using are not native to SQL Server.

Open Data Services can be used to integrate other data sources

At the heart of SQL Server is a programming language called Transact-SQL. Transact-SQL is an extension of standard SQL, with programming language constructs such as variables, loops, procedures, triggers, and rules. A procedure written in Transact-SQL can be stored in the DBMS and invoked by request.

Transact-SQL is SQL Server's proprietary language

Triggers, on the other hand, can be used to enforce referential integrity and to perform many data validation tasks. For example, if you had an employee table with a salary column, a trigger could be written to make sure that the salary amount stayed within a certain range. If an application tried to insert a salary amount outside if that range, the trigger would initiate some sort of corrective action. This is a very elegant solution to data validation, because it avoids having to build this type of logic into every application that uses the table.

Triggers can be used for data validation and referential integrity

Application Development Tools

For someone coming from a mainframe background, the number and variety of tools available for client/server development can be very overwhelming and confusing. It's truly a jungle out there! Some typical questions are: "Should we use C or a 4GL?" "Whose product is the best for what we are trying to do?" "Will the performance be acceptable for this application?"

A large number of client/server tools already exists

We will attempt to provide answers to some of these questions, or at least some helpful insights. Client/server applications can be built using a variety of programming languages and development tools.

Tool selection criteria include your experience and the user's task

Which tool to use is largely a matter of:

- Your background. If you and your team are system-oriented programmers with some experience in languages such as C or PL/1, you might be more inclined to continue to use these languages. On the other hand, if your background is oriented to application programming, you would be more inclined to use a 4GL like Visual Basic, PowerBuilder, SQLWindows, or ObjectView.

- Target Audience. If you are developing code libraries or system level components where performance and efficiency are of paramount importance, chances are that you will use a compiled language like C or C++. On the other hand, if you are assembling applications for end users for internal use or resale, you probably will favor higher level languages and tools.

4GLs

Let's examine 4GLs

Traditional programming languages such as C, COBOL, PL/1, and FORTRAN have been extensively written about and used. Therefore, in this section we will focus on facilities provided by 4GLs. We will then examine one of the most popular tools used in client/server development—Powersoft's PowerBuilder.

4GLs simplify developing GUI applications

Over the last several years, a large number of GUI front end tools have emerged on the marketplace. These 4GLs provide users with the ability to develop GUI applications quickly and painlessly. I say *painlessly*, because programming to a native GUI API (using Microsoft's SDK, for example) is a very tedious and time-consuming process for an application programmer. To be productive, an application programmer must be able to build GUI applications in a very short amount of time, even if some flexibility and efficiency must be given up.

The GUI front end building tools fall into at least three categories:

Categorizing GUI building tools

- *General GUI building tools*   The tools in this category are designed for building any kind of GUI application. They provide standard user interface objects such as list boxes, push buttons, pull down menus, etc. The leading tool in this category is Microsoft's Visual Basic.

- *Database front end tools*   These GUI building tools also offer a set of user interface objects, but are more geared toward developing front end applications to database management systems. They often integrate data derived from DBMSs into visual objects. All such tools come with a built-in stand-alone database engine. The most popular tools in this category are Power-Builder, SQLWindows and ObjectView.

- *Screen scrapers*   These GUI building tools offer facilities to existing front end terminal applications (mostly IBM's 3270) with a new GUI interface. They work by reading dataflows to and from existing terminal-oriented applications. Some of the more popular tools in this category are FlashPoint and Mozart.

Example: PowerBuilder

Over the last several years, Powersoft's PowerBuilder has become a very popular database front end building tool. It has developed a reputation for ease of use and robustness.

PowerBuilder is a popular tool

PowerBuilder applications are built using a variety of *painters*:

- Application Painter is used to define general details about an application, such as its name, the libraries used and their search paths, and application icons.

Painters define application characteristics,

- Window Painter creates windows and window controls such as push buttons and radio buttons. Through Window Painter, a programmer can control the window size, title, borders, scroll bars, and visibility. Using a very intuitive tool bar, a programmer can select virtually any user interface object available in Windows. By clicking on, say, a push button icon, a programmer can create a push button anywhere on the screen. A *script* can be attached to any user interface control. A script is a segment of Basic-like code in PowerBuilder's language (PowerScript). Each user interface control has a number of events associated with it. Examples of events are *clicks* or *double-clicks*. Scripts are associated with specific events; when an event occurs, a script gets executed.

windows,

menus,	• Menu Painter is used to create a menu bar for any application window. The top level action bar items can be defined, along with other submenu items.
database access,	• DataWindow Painter is a special kind of object that acts as the primary control for data interaction with a DBMS. DataWindows can interact with data coming from SQL selects, SQL queries, stored procedures, or even an external function in a dynamic link library. Once a data source is selected, a SQL painter can be used to generate a query. This query can be reused in other data windows or objects, if so desired. To make sure that only good data come into the system, a set of data validation criteria can also be associated with a data window. Before a data window object can be used to display data, it must be associated with a data window control object. This object is the user interface to a data window. It controls things like colors, fonts, window position, and so on.
variables,	• Structure Painter can be used to create and change structures. A structure is a group of variables used together to represent some common data element. Structures are a very familiar concept to C programmers. To COBOL programmers, structures are records defined at a common level (05, for example).
SQL queries,	• Query Painter allows a programmer to visually create a SQL query. A programmer can pick tables, specify join conditions, display formats, set validation criteria, and so on.
on-line help,	• Help Painter is used to create an on-line help system.
user-defined objects,	• Object Painter is used to create a custom control. Once created, this control is treated like any other PowerBuilder control. Although most custom controls are user interface-related, a non-user interface object can be created to capture some reusable application behavior.
and function selection	• Function Painter simplifies the selection of PowerBuilder built-in functions.

Building a PowerBuilder Application

The first step in building a PowerBuilder application is to define some basic application details in the application. Several important events like OPEN, CLOSE, and IDLE can be intercepted by your application. For example, an OPEN event would typically include a line like `open(w_first_window)` that displays the initial application window. Other initialization-related code can be added to the OPEN event script.

First, basic application details are defined in Application Painter

The next step is to use Window Painter to create one or more windows for your application. A window will contain a set of controls with which the user will interact. At the heart of every PowerBuilder application is the data window control. It is the primary way for a PowerBuilder application to interface with a database. Other painters create application windows, variables, SQL, and so on.

Once an application is built, it can be compiled to an executable module. This executable file can run outside of the PowerBuilder environment, as long as the run-time DLLs that come with PowerBuilder can be found.

PowerBuilder applications can be made into executable code

4GLs Versus 3GLs

Which language/development tool you will use is one of the most important decisions you will have to make. There is no single "right" answer. Unfortunately the real answer is the proverbial—"it depends."

The choice of development tools depends on many factors

There is a wide variety of development tools. Each tool has its strengths and weaknesses. Perhaps the most fundamental decision one has to make is whether to use a *fourth-generation language* (4GL). 4GLs have reemerged in the client/server world as tools designed to speed up the application development process. They are typically targeted to solve problems in a specific domain, such as database applications. The decision to use a 4GL is based on what you value.

4GLs have pluses and minuses

The primary strengths of a 4GL are the following:

4GL strengths

- Ease of development and high productivity. Most 4GLs aim at solving problems in a particular domain. As such, they come with many "building blocks" already assembled and ready to be used.

- Shorter development time. Given that programmers can work at a higher level of abstraction, a program should take less time to write.

- Since many building blocks come standard with a 4GL, a programmer does not need to know many low level details of an operating system or a database. Thus, a less technical programmer could build these applications.

- Possibly improved portability. I say *possibly* because the portability of a 4GL application really depends on the vendor's ability and willingness to port the language to many operating systems. For example, Progress software, a 4GL/database vendor, assures its customers of application portability to many different platforms. For many smaller firms involved in a vertical application development market, this message is very appealing. These vendors simply do not have the financial and programming resources to port or exploit many different operating systems on their own.

4GL drawbacks   Of course, 4GLs have many significant drawbacks:

- Proprietary language. If you decide that you don't like your vendor any more, you can't "pick up" your code and move to another development tool. For the most part, 4GLs are proprietary languages and thus are supported only by a single vendor.

- Unacceptable performance. 4GLs typically require extensive runtime support, which takes up additional memory and CPU cycles. Such support comes in the form of one or many large *dynamic link libraries* in the Windows and OS/2 environments. When a 4GL application runs, the code in these DLLs gets loaded into system's memory, possibly causing excessive paging and eventually affecting performance.

     Another common source of performance problems comes from the 4GLs' need to support a variety of DBMSs. To do that, they typically resort to the lowest common denominator, and do not take advantage of the performance-oriented features that are unique to each DBMS.

Finally, many 4GLs generate less efficient interpretive code which runs significantly slower than compiled code generated by languages such as C, C++, or COBOL.

- Many 4GLs impose a particular type of client/server architecture. Your flexibility as a designer of a system is constrained by the 4GL's support of modularization. For example, should you decide that a particular function really needs to execute on the server instead of a client machine, your ability to distribute processing of this function to another machine is limited.

- Less flexibility. The very fact that 4GLs are so productive limits your choices—many decisions have already been made for you, whether you like them or not.

- 4GLs are not computationally complete. Many 4GLs are specialized languages designed solely to handle a particular domain, such as database manipulation. A 4GL may not have the constructs that are needed to handle nondatabase activity, forcing you to extend the tool with home-grown functions typically written in C or C++.

Third-generation languages (3GLs) such a C, COBOL, and Basic in many ways have just the opposite strengths and weaknesses. Their strengths are:

3GLs also have pluses…

- Efficient and fast code. 3GLs are, for the most part, compiled languages. The executables of such languages consist of low level machine instruction that can be executed by a CPU without any additional translation.

- Ability to fully express any computing needs, i.e., computational completeness.

- Portability between and support on many hardware platforms and operating systems. 3GLs such as COBOL and C have been standardized to a large extent. For example, the C run-time library is the same regardless of the operating system where an application runs. Thus, very few code changes are necessary to port an application from one system to another.

…and minuses

And as far as the weaknesses go,

- It takes longer to develop applications with 3GLs than with 4GLs. Many low-level and time-consuming details must be taken care of by application code.

- 3GLs are more difficult to learn, and require more technically skilled programmers.

Use 3GLs for performance and 4GLs for programmer productivity

If high performance, asset preservation, flexibility, and portability are important to you, then you should use a 3GL like C. If you care more about programmer productivity and don't mind paying a little extra for more powerful hardware, perhaps a 4GL will serve you well.

Often a combination of 3GLs and 4GLs is the right choice

The most important point that I want to convey is that this decision is not an *either–or* proposition. Many successful large-scale distributed systems have been written using a combination of 4GL and 3GL tools. For example, a user interface component is best written in a 4GL, because it can save a lot of time. A multiuser server is best written in a 3GL, because it provides efficient, compiled code.

Suggested Reading

C. J. Date, *An Introduction to Database Systems,* Reading: Addison Wesley, 1986.

Koch and Muller, *Oracle 7: The Complete Reference,* New York: McGraw Hill, 1993.

C. J. Date, *A Guide to DB2,* Reading: Addison Wesley, 1984.

Microsoft SQL Server, Redmond: Microsoft Press, 1992.

Parsaye, Chignell, Khoshfian, and Wong, *Intelligent Databases,* New York: Wiley, 1989.

9

Groupware

Over the last several years, a new class of software has emerged known as *groupware*. Groupware is a broad term that describes a simple idea—personal computers connected on the network can serve as a medium of information storage and exchange for people working on a common task.

Groupware enables cooperation

As the concept of a *virtual* corporation is taking hold, where employees are dispersed throughout the globe, groupware is increasingly seen as the backbone of the virtual office infrastructure that allows people to work together.

It is especially appealing now

There are many examples of tasks that are group oriented. The most universal ones are scheduling meetings, sending electronic mail, and exchanging documents. These functions must be performed in a group setting, because they involve a group of people. For example, the electronic mail process requires at least two individuals—the sender and the intended receiver.

Common groupware functions

In addition to these universal groupware applications, more specialized uses of groupware concepts also exist. For example, it is very common for a group of engineers to collaborate on the design of, say, an automobile. Such collaboration entails sharing and reviewing of drawings, specification documents—even CAD/CAM files. An easy way to think about how all of this information is stored is by envisioning it contained in a virtual folder.

There are lots of more specialized groupware needs

What technical components are used to implement this virtual work folder? The most fundamental component is messaging. Through messaging, information can flow from one computer to another (Figure 9.1).

Electronic messaging is the foundation

Two types of messaging needed for groupware communication are: real-time and store-and-forward. In real-time messaging, information is transferred immediately from the sender to the receiver. For example,

Messaging is real-time or store-and-forward (e-mail)

when a user of a scheduling application wants to check the availability of a conference room, he or she must receive an instantaneous response to the query. Both the sender of the message and its receiver have to be running when the messages are sent.

Figure 9.1   Messaging

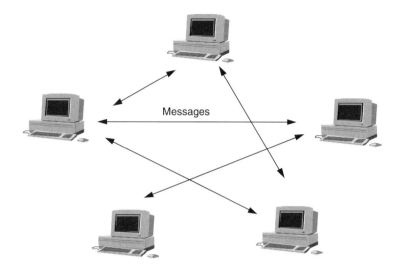

Messages

E-mail is a form of messaging

For tasks that are not so time critical, or where the receiving of messages can take place at different times (e.g., e-mail), a store-and-forward type of messaging is needed. As its name implies, a message is moved from the sender to the receiver, or to an intermediate computer, and subsequently gets stored. The storage can also take place on the sender's machine if the connection with the receiver cannot be established. The store-and-forward process continues until the message gets received at the destination.

Another important component is a shared database

The storage of messages and other forms of data brings us to another fundamental component of every groupware solution—a database. A database stores information which will be shared with others. For example, in a meeting scheduling system, the calendars of every individual and that of all the meeting rooms are stored in a database, so that every authorized user can schedule meetings with other users.

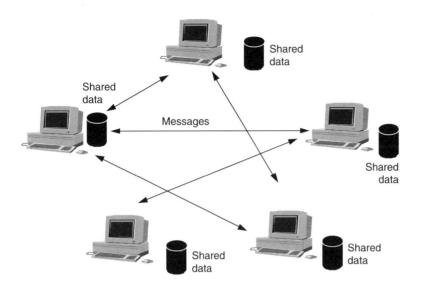

Figure 9.2   Groupware
technology components—
messaging and shared data

The storage of shared data can occur on many computers (Figure 9.2). One of the distinguishing characteristics of groupware is that information must be available to any user, regardless of location. This requirement is often met by replicating data across at least several machines. This process insures both high availability of data and proximity to the requester for improved access and performance.

Data must be universally available

Another crucial requirement for any groupware system is to be able to access data in other DBMS systems and legacy applications (Figure 9.3). A groupware database cannot be an island of information. It must connect to and exchange information with other sources of data in a company.

Access to all data sources is needed

Other sources of data can include an existing DBMS, legacy systems, and data warehouses. It is important to note that such data exchanges must take place bidirectionally. A one-way dataflow in or out of a groupware database is only sufficient if the groupware application uses or creates read-only data. If the application is used for important operational needs of the business, chances are that the created data need to be included in the overall system dataflow process.

A bidirectional exchange of data to legacy systems is often needed

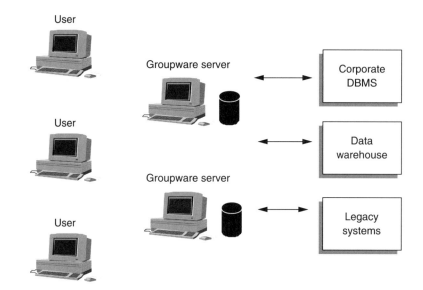

Figure 9.3 Groupware must exchange data with other DBMS and legacy systems

User

Groupware server

Corporate DBMS

User

Data warehouse

Groupware server

User

Legacy systems

Workflow Systems

Workflow is a special case of groupware

Closely associated with groupware is the term *workflow management.* In fact, workflow management is a special case of a groupware solution. Some tasks, such as collaborative design, can be performed by individuals at any time, without much structure or predefined rules needed to perform the task. For example, a group of engineers collaborating on a design of a new car can be seen as an unstructured process. Each engineer adds to the design when and if he or she comes up with an idea or an improvement on an existing component.

Workflow is geared towards structured activities

Other groupware tasks require a lot of structure, rules, and procedures that must be followed. Such tasks usually involve the transfer of ownership or control of the task as it moves from one person to another. The process is similar to a conveyer in an assembly line, where the product gets moved from one group to another until it gets completed.

Example: purchase order processing

For example, a purchase order approval process is a groupware task with a very well-defined sequence of steps. First, the purchase order goes to a manager, who then might have to forward it to a supervisor if the amount is beyond his or her signing authority, and so on. This is an example where workflow management groupware would be an appropriate solution.

There are many good groupware products on the market today. Let's take a closer look at Lotus Notes to gain appreciation for what a groupware product can do and how it works.

Groupware products

Example: Lotus Notes

Lotus Notes is a groupware system designed for capturing and disseminating information. It has some characteristics of a database, but with one major difference. Notes treats information as a constantly changing entity which cannot be bound by a set of rigidly defined tables and columns of relational databases. Instead, Notes data structures can change right along with the data in them (Figure 9.4).

Notes is designed to disseminate information

Notes stores data in databases, that are in turn made up of documents. A database is equivalent to a folder containing documents. A document roughly maps into a relational database's record. A document consists of fields. These fields can contain structured and unstructured data, such as text, graphics, images, and other data types.

Documents make up Notes databases

Relational database

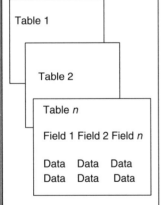

Notes database

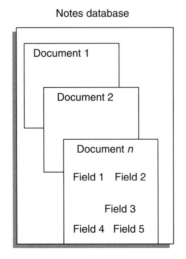

Figure 9.4 Relational database versus Notes database

Users can create and update documents by using forms. Forms display the fields of a document, and in many ways resemble printed

Forms are used to manipulate documents

paper forms. The fields can be entered or updated with multiple choice selections, graphics, and other design elements. A document can be viewed through a number of different forms.

Views filter out documents

Since a database can potentially consist of thousands of documents, there must be some way to select only these documents that the user is interested in. This is accomplished by views (Figure 9.5). The word *view* is somewhat misleading. Views are not used to observe the contents of documents (that is, the function of a forms), but to organize the documents in a user-desired order.

Views sort documents in a desired order

A view is similar to a table of contents in a book. It shows the documents as chapters and topics that are available for viewing. If the user wants to actually view a certain document, a form is displayed.

Figure 9.5   Notes views and forms

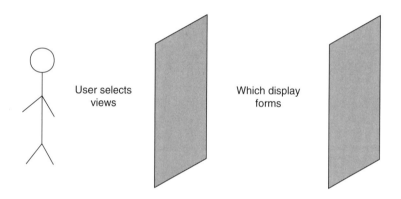

User selects views

Which display forms

Notes is a distributed application

Lotus Notes is a distributed client/server application. It consists of client and server components which can communicate through a number of different networks. A client component runs in every user's computer. A Notes database can be either local or shared. Local databases physically reside on users' machines and do not require any support from the server.

Shared databases are stored on servers

If a database is to be shared with a group of people (which is often the case), it must be stored on the server. A server makes a database accessible to all authorized users. A server is also responsible for database management tasks such as database compaction, index updates, logging, and so on.

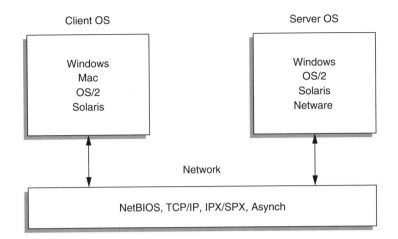

Figure 9.6 Notes-supported platforms and networks

Client OS

Windows
Mac
OS/2
Solaris

Server OS

Windows
OS/2
Solaris
Netware

Network

NetBIOS, TCP/IP, IPX/SPX, Asynch

Customizing Notes

Notes is a general-purpose information sharing facility. Right out of the box, it comes with a number of applications such as call tracking and group discussion. Until release 3.0, extendibility of Notes to handle other tasks was weak. The 3.0 release of Notes significantly improved the programmability of Notes, thus allowing its users to build customized applications with very little effort. Many users of Notes still do not realize that it can be used as an application development environment and not just as a discussion database.

Notes can easily be customized to handle many tasks

Notes can be tailored to many information tracking and workflow applications with very little *spreadsheet macro-like* programming. Its built-in e-mail facilities enable workflow types of applications, where forms can be routed or mailed to people around the company. Some examples of successfully implemented Notes applications include:

Notes offers a macro-like language

- Customer support

- Small inventory tracking and reporting

- Problem management systems

- Résumé tracking

A programmer first creates forms, and adds fields to them	Notes applications are built by first creating one or more forms. When creating a new form, a programmer can create a number of fields that will reside on the form. There are many different types of fields that can be created. For example, a programmer can designate fields as numeric, textual, graphic, OLE object, and so on. One can think of these fields as variables. Some fields can be shared between multiple forms, and are used like global variables.
Code is added to fields	Once a field is created, a segment of code can be "attached" to it that describes how the field will receive its value. The Notes term for this segment of code is a *formula*. Formulas can be used to:

- Assign a value or calculate a value for a field
- Perform a conversion on data
- Select a subset of documents for display in a view
- Validate input data

Notes functions	Formulas can consist of one or more @ functions. Some examples of @ functions include:

```
@MailSend
@Hour
@If
@DBLookUp
@Command
@DDEInitiate
```

Formula selection is the bulk of development	There are several hundred such @ functions. As you have probably guessed, the majority of effort in building a customized Notes application involves selecting and combining the @ functions to achieve the desired results.
Products like Notes can be used to build custom applications and to avoid building systems from scratch	Lotus Notes and other groupware products are increasingly becoming customizable. With a little bit of programming, these products can be used to build fairly complex distributed systems. In fact, such products should be thought of as a set of building blocks which can be tailored to assemble systems quickly. Naturally, not every type of distributed system can be built with tools like Notes, but where appropriate, it can serve as a powerful alternative to building systems from the ground up.

Suggested Reading

Getting Started with Application Developement: Lotus Notes Server Release 3, Lotus Developement Corporation Part Number 12601, Cambridge, MA, 1993. Contact Lotus at (617) 693-8965.

10

Distributed Application Models

Among all the technical reasons why some distributed applications fail to meet user expectations, one clearly stands out—poor application architecture. A poor architectural decision is likely to surface as a system that is consistently slow, unreliable, and hard to maintain. What makes architectural problems so difficult to correct is that there are no easy fix-up solutions to them. It is like having a house built, and then deciding that a staircase should have been placed in another room.

Poor application architecture results in problems that are difficult to correct

In order to successfully deliver distributed systems, a thorough analysis must be undertaken to determine which distributed system's architecture is the most appropriate. This chapter should help you answer questions like:

The application architecture must be determined up front

- What are the DBMS requirements needed to build high-volume multiuser applications?

- How can you fully exploit a distributed DBMS? What are the advantages and disadvantages of screen scraping?

- Do you have to resort to network programming in order to implement a good distributed system?

- How can you partition applications into client and servers? What criteria should be used to do that?

- How can you ensure the scalability of your system as the number of users, their locations, and volume grow?

Understanding the Network

To answer some of these questions, we must take a closer look at the network. Consider the internal speed of a personal computer. It can range from 10 to 20 Mbytes per second for processor-to-memory

Network speed in relation to other speeds

communication, and from 1 to 2 Mbytes per second to I/O devices. In contrast, the speed of a local area network is at least an order of magnitude slower (Figure 10.1).

Figure 10.1 Relative speeds of various system components

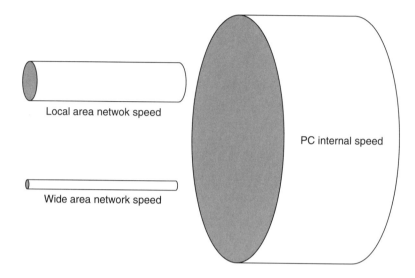

Local area netwok speed

PC internal speed

Wide area network speed

The network can quickly become a bottleneck

A 4-Mbit-per-second token ring network can theoretically transfer data 4 million bits per second. After this number is rounded off to bytes and the overhead of a transport protocol is subtracted, the effective network throughput is on the order of 100 to 200 Kbytes per second. That is at least an order of magnitude slower than internal computer speed! This simple fact is often overlooked.

Minimize Network Trips

Coupling processes with data is advantageous

Common sense tells us that when designing distributed applications, network communications between application components should be kept to a minimum. One way to reduce the network traffic is to place data and the code that manipulates them on the same machine. This way, instead of sending many requests across the network for data and then manipulating them, your application sends a single request to perform a certain function. In the latter scenario, there is a single round-trip (Figure 10.2).

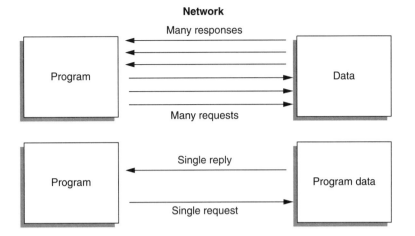

Figure 10.2 Coupling code and data minimizes the number of network trips

Another way to minimize the number of network trips is to make use of data caching techniques. Caching techniques work around the simple principle of access locality. Put in simple terms, if data were accessed once, there is a good chance that they will be accessed again, and the chance of adjacent data being accessed also increases.

Caching relies on access locality

If this assumption holds true, distributed systems can take advantage of that fact by transferring more data across the network than are actually needed to satisfy the current request and storing them in a local cache. The hope is that subsequent requests can be satisfied out of the cache, without having to make additional network trips.

Caching can minimize network activity

Fat Versus Thin Clients

During client/server application design meetings, one of the most hotly contested issues is how to determine whether to have thin clients and fat servers, or fat clients and thin servers. Here, *thinness* and *fatness* have to do with the relative amount of code residing in the client and server components.

Fatness versus thinness

When examining this issue with the speed of the network in mind, it becomes obvious that there is no clear cut answer. Instead, designers should examine each function of a system, and decide where the data it needs should reside. There are a number of factors that should be considered during this decision.

Code partitioning depends on the details

Six Principles of Function Placement

The following principles should guide your decisions on function placement:

Frequency and scope are often at odds

- *Frequency and scope*   The first principle involves the frequency and scope of a particular function. By *scope,* I mean how widely the function is used. The greater the number of functions that call a particular function, the greater its scope. If a given function is used by many other functions, we can say that the function has a broad scope. In the context of a distributed system design, scope and frequency are sometimes at odds with each other. Intuition tells us that if a function is used frequently, it should be placed as close to its caller as possible to eliminate the network delay, but if the function also happens to be used widely, one can argue that it belongs in a server. After all, by placing it in the server, the client code size is reduced, and sharing of the function increases.

Don't separate processes and data

- *Location of data*   The second principle has already been stated. If the data are available only on the server machine, placing a particular function in a client component does not make sense. In such a case, it would be better to move the function over to the server in order to eliminate the need for multiple data requests on the network.

Availability of processing cycles

- *Process allocation*   The third principle is overall balance of processing power. Since the components of a system execute on separate processors in the network, an obvious question should be asked: "Is the workload among the processors being evenly distributed?" This issue is important because the overall system performance is a function of all of the system components.

Every system executes at the speed of its slowest component

It takes only one component to slow down the entire system. Put another way, the system will perform at the speed of its slowest component. The goal is to make sure that the application evenly distributes processing among all components and takes advantage of every processor in the network.

- *Application development tool*   The choice of application development tool is also important. Some environments can be used to create dynamically linked libraries; therefore all functions written in such tools can be shared only in that language environment. For example, it would be difficult to write a server component which processes hundreds of concurrent user requests in a tool like Smalltalk. The overhead of dynamic languages like Smalltalk, in terms of memory requirements and code efficiency would not make it the best choice for the job. On the other hand, Smalltalk would make a great tool for writing the user interface component of a system.

  The language environment determines code partitioning

- *Code reusability*   Another principle of function placement is code reusability. Physically, there are two ways to achieve code reusability. First, a function can be placed in a server and accessed by all client applications through a *remote procedure call* (RPC).

  Two approaches to code reusability

  This approach has the advantage of reducing the code size of application components that call the function. Another advantage is that there is only one place where the function needs to be changed. The disadvantage of placing the function in the server is the network delay that is incurred on every call.

  The server approach reduces code size

  The second way to achieve code reusability, which minimizes the network delay, is to place the function in a common code library that is statically or dynamically linked to all application components. This is a more traditional approach to code reusability, but it is still applicable to distributed systems.

  A code library minimizes the number of network trips

- *Application concurrency*   Function placement also should be based on application concurrency. We often think about our programs as executing serially, one instruction at a time. If a program performs functions *A*, *B*, *C*, and *D*, it does so sequentially—i.e., *A*, then *B*, then *C*, and so on. Having a network of processors presents a designer with the opportunity to use them in parallel. In fact, a network of computers can be thought of as a multiprocessor machine. If a given set of business functions lends itself to parallel execution, the overall system performance can be improved.

  Networked applications can execute many functions in parallel

Consider the example in Figure 10.3, where a physical database has been alphabetically split up between four machines, and contains customer-related information. A request to find all customers with orders outstanding for more than sixty days can be performed simultaneously on the four machines. All four machines can perform the same request, because there is no dependency between the data elements. The results of these requests are combined on the client and presented to a user.

Figure 10.3 Parallel database lookup

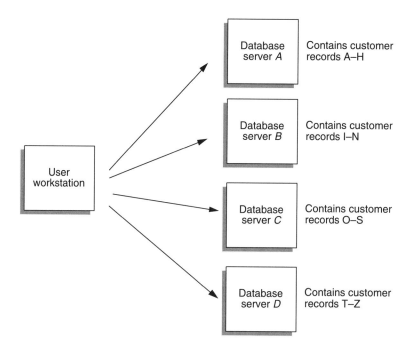

Distributed Application Models

Let's examine common networked models

Equipped with the six principles of function placement, we can better evaluate commonly used networked application architectures. Our discussion should help you decide which architectural model is the most appropriate for your project.

Essentially, five models are used in building distributed systems. These models differ in how the network is being used and where the *network split* in the application code takes place. Each model has its strengths and weaknesses. The important thing is to understand what those strengths and weaknesses are.

Before explaining the five models in detail, let's take a look at a typical monolithic application structure we have grown to know and love. A typical application consists of a user interface code, a business logic code, and a data management code.

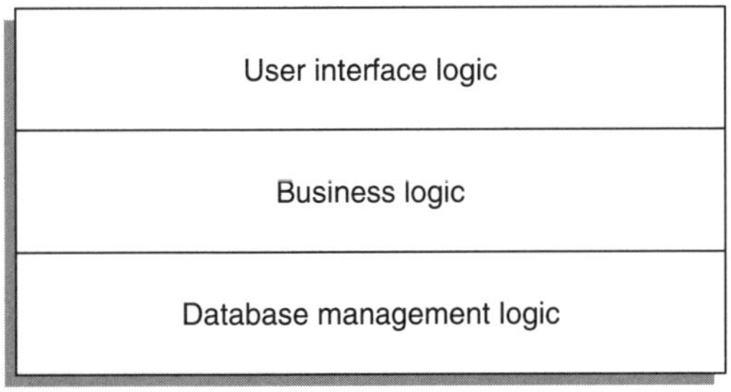

Figure 10.4 Typical application structure

| User interface logic |
| Business logic |
| Database management logic |

The user interface code naturally deals with the user interface tasks, i.e., presenting data in windows, getting user input, and performing field validation. It is the component most familiar to the users of the system.

The rules of the business and its computations—essentially the "guts" of every program—reside in the business logic section of the code. The code in this section defines the functionality of the system.

The data management section contains code that manipulates files and databases. It is responsible for storing and retrieving application data.

The five models presented here (Figure 10.5) differ in how the application structure is split up into client and server components. Let's examine each model in more detail.

Figure 10.5 Distributed
application models

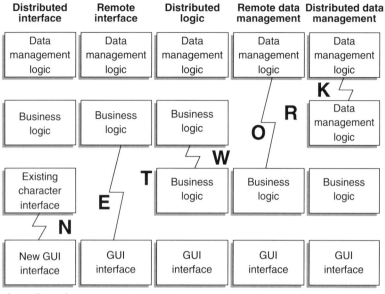

Distributed interface	Remote interface	Distributed logic	Remote data management	Distributed data management
Data management logic	Data management logic	Data management logic	Data management logic	Data management logic
Business logic	Business logic	Business logic		Data management logic
Existing character interface		Business logic	Business logic	Business logic
New GUI interface	GUI interface	GUI interface	GUI interface	GUI interface

Source: Gartner Group

The Distributed Interface Model

The distributed interface involves adding a GUI front end

This model, also known as *screen scraping,* is typically the first attempt at network enabling of an old mainframe application. It involves building another user interface, most likely a graphical one, in front of an existing *dumb terminal* interface. In the IBM mainframe world, the terminal interface is commonly known as a 3270-style interface. The 3270-style interface is what a user sees when working with a terminal connected to the mainframe.

It gives applications a new look

A GUI is added to an existing application to make it user-friendly. It is a quick way to turn an application that is hard to use, due to its cryptic commands or data-packed screens, into an easy-to-use, modern application.

Available tools

There are a number of tools in the marketplace that can be used to build GUI 3270 front end applications. Some popular ones are Flash-Point, Easel, and Mozart.

Technical Details of 3270 Screen Scraping

To help you understand the limits of what is possible with *front end-ing,* we need to explore the technical details behind it. All screen scraping tools require some form of 3270 emulation package. A 3270 emulator is software that turns a personal computer into a dumb terminal. More specifically, it knows how to send and receive the 3270 data streams (Figure 10.6).

All screen scraping tools work on a 3270 data stream

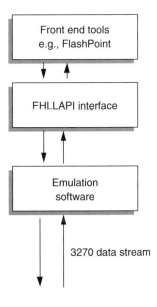

Figure 10.6   3270 front ending

Just about all 3270 emulators offer a programming interface to any PC application. This interface is known as the *emulator high level language application programming interface* (EHLLAPI). EHLLAPI has become the de facto standard way for a PC application to interact with a 3270 screen, and therefore is used by may front end tools.

EHLLAPI is a standard API

It is important to understand EHLLAPI's capabilities, because they determine what can be accomplished using screen scraping. The first important concept to understand is that EHLLAPI is a programming interface for interacting with host screens. In fact, you should think of your EHLLAPI program as a fast typist. All of the EHLLAPI commands deal with screen manipulation.

EHLLAPI programming involves programming to screens

In EHLLAPI terms, a host screen is known as a *presentation space*. A presentation space is equivalent to a mainframe session. Each presentation name is known by its short name: *A, B, C,* and so on. The following tables lists some EHLLAPI functions and their descriptions:

Connect Presentation Space	Establishes a connection between your application and a 3270 session
Copy Field to String	Copies characters at a specified screen position to a string
Copy Presentation Space	Copies the contents of the host-connected presentation space into application's data buffer
Copy Presentation Space to String	Copies all or part of a host-connected presentation space to your program
Copy String to Field	Copies a string to a location (field) in a 3270 screen
Copy String to Presentation Space	Copies an ASCII string to a location specified in a presentation space
Disconnect Presentation Space	Disconnects an application from a presentation space
Find Field Position	Returns the starting position of a field in a presentation space
Get Key	Allows application to intercept keystrokes specified by the Start Keystroke Intercept Function
PAUSE	Waits for a specified period of time or a specified host event.
Query Session Status	Returns session-specific information
Query Sessions	Returns the number of started host sessions

Query System	Returns emulator system data
Receive File	Used to transfer a session from a host to workstation
Search Field	Searches the current presentation space fields for a specified string
Search Presentation Space	Searches the entire presentation space for a string
Send File	Transfers a file from a workstation to host
Send Key	Sends one or a series of keystrokes to a presentation space
Set Cursor	Sets the position of the cursor within a presentation space
Set Session Parameters	Configures session options in EHLLAPI
Wait	Checks on the presentation space. If the host uses xclock, this function causes EHLLAPI to wait

Using EHLLAPI, an application can query session status, send data to the host, upload and download files, and search the screens for specific data or fields. All EHLLAPI functions are accessible through a single function call, HLLC, and take the following parameters:

All functions are accessed through one entry point

- *Function number* Function number of a EHLLAPI command (listed in the middle column)

- *Data string* Used primarily to send and receive a data string

- *Data string length or buffer size* Indicates the size of the data string

- *Host presentation space position* PS position. The maximum PS position is 1920.

After the call completes, the four parameters contain returned information as follows:

- *Function number*   Remains unchanged

- *Data string*   Varies with function. Typically returns a string of characters

- *Data sting length, PS position or attribute value*   Usually returns a length of returned data

- *Return code*   Indicates the success or failure of a function

EHLLAPI Coding Example in C

Coding example

Here is an example of a C function that calls EHLLAPI to find a string, CUSTOMER NAME, on the host screen.

```c
#include <stdio.h>
#include <string.h>
int find_string()
{
  short  function_number=6;          /* search PS space code */
  char   data_string[256];
  short  data_string_length;
  short  return_code=0;              /* start searching at PS 0 */

  strcpy(data_string, "CUSTOMER NAME");
  data_string_length = strlen(data_string);

  /* call EHLLAPI */
  hllc(&function_number, data_string, &data_string_length, &
      &return_code);

  if ( return_code == 0 )            /* string was not found */
     printf("\nString: CUSTOMER NAME not found\n");
  else
     printf("\nString found at position %i\n", return_code);
}
```

Example explained

The strcpy line copies the string CUSTOMER NAME to the data_string variable, and the next line sets the length parameter to the length of that string. The following lines show how EHLLAPI is called. If the code returned in return_code is equal to 0, the string was not found. Otherwise, the string was found at the location returned in data_string_length.

Advantages of the Distributed Interface Model

- This approach does not require any changes to the mainframe application, which is one of its major advantages. The new GUI interface acts as the "user" to the old interface. It translates user mouse clicks and selections into commands that the old mainframe interface can recognize, and redisplays output data using GUI widgets.

- Another advantage to this approach is that it can "combine" multiple 3270 screens into one or more GUI windows, thus making the user interface not only easier to use, but also easier to navigate.

- Replacing a large mainframe application that has been around for many years is not an easy task. To minimize this effort, a multiphased approach with screen scraping can make the replacement more gradual. The first phase might encompass a new GUI front end and some PC code. Subsequent releases could continue to add PC code while replacing mainframe system components.

Disadvantages

- One major disadvantage is that "coding" to screens is not a very robust way of building networked applications. If any screen changes are made to an existing mainframe system, the screen scraper applications need to be modified.

  Some changes in the 3270 data stream can impact the front end applications. For instance, such changes could result from adding 3270 data compression products.

- Another drawback to front ending, is that it does not take full advantage of the local area network environment, and it underutilizes the power of personal computers for groupware activities. In fact, a local area network does not even have to exist for screen scraping applications. Any personal computer connected as a dumb terminal to a cluster controller (e.g., 3x74) by a coaxial cable can support a screen scraping application.

- Screen scraped applications can also affect network traffic. Combining or searching through multiple 3270 screens and changing how the user interacts with a system can increase the number of 3270 screens being sent (1920 bytes each), and thus increase network traffic.

Screen scraping is a good first step

Despite its disadvantages, if your objective is to improve an existing 3270 application without investing a lot of money towards its redesign, and also to deliver some improvements to the users quickly, screen scraping is a reasonable approach.

The Remote Interface Model

The remote interface can execute on another machine

This model decouples the user interface component from the rest of the application, and thus enables the user interface to execute on another processor in the network. The most prominent example of the remote interface model is the X Window system developed at the Massachusetts Institute of Technology. Using X Window, an application can run its user interface on any computer in the network.

Figure 10.7   Remote interface model

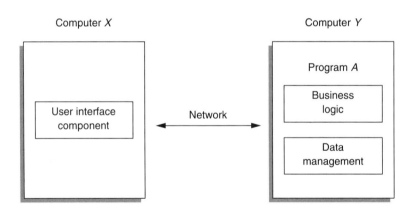

Example of remote interface

In Figure 10.7, program *A* is running on system *Y,* but has its user interface on system *X.* As the program executes, it sends user interface commands to system *X,* which in turn displays them. Similarly, user actions are forwarded from system *X* to system *Y,* where program *A* can act on them.

In X Window terminology, the application is called a *client*. Clients communicate with X servers which perform user interface functions. In our example, system *X* acts a server. This terminology can be confusing, because most people think of clients as the requesters of services, and servers as the providers. They typically associate a client component with providing the user interface function and a server with taking care of the rest.

In X Window, a client is an application

In some ways, the traditional terminal I/O style of centralized systems could be classified as a remote interface style application. If you think about how a host CICS application interacts with a user, you can argue that it uses remote interface functionality. Of course, the big difference is that the terminal is a nonintelligent device, and therefore a passive player in the network.

A remote interface is similar to having terminals

Advantages

One advantage of decoupling a user interface component from the rest of the application is that it allows both the user interface and the remainder of the system to change and still be able to communicate with each other. The important thing here is to preserve the interfaces through which this communication takes place.

Another advantage of separating off the user interface is that the needs of various users of the system can be better addressed. In a large scale application, it is often desirable to have a couple of different interfaces on the system, in order to reflect the needs of users performing a variety of tasks. By separating the interface component out, this option becomes possible.

In some cases a user interface is not a set of windows on a user's machine. A user interface could be a fax machine, a telephone, or another communication device directly linked to the system (Figure 10.8).

Separating the user interface from the rest of the system also allows the users to interact with other distributed systems (Figure 10.9).

Figure 10.8 Variety of remote interfaces

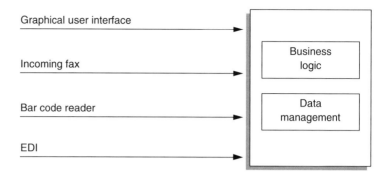

In fact, the best way to think about the user interface component in the distributed world is as a window into the entire computing environment. Such a computing environment need not be comprised only of the company's own resources, but can extend to other companies and global networks. In the age of corporate mergers and consolidations, the ability to unify divergent systems is not only desirable, but often mandatory.

Figure 10.9 User interface to multiple systems

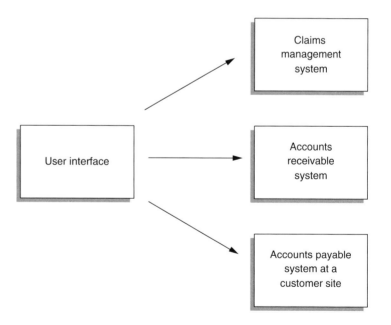

The user who interacts with a system should not be aware of other systems that are involved in performing his or her tasks. Such system-to-system interaction should remain totally transparent.

Disadvantages

The primary disadvantage of the remote interface model has to do with the amount of network traffic it generates. The X Window environment is a perfect example of that. The original implementation of X sent just about every user action as a separate message. Just imagine how many messages would be sent if a user moved the mouse from one corner to another. Many later implementations of X compensated for this deficiency by bundling several low level messages into larger messages.

The important point here is that maintaining communication between the user interface and the rest of the system at too granular a level can create a lot of network traffic. As indicated earlier in this chapter, the speed of the network, more specifically the wide area network speed, is still relatively slow when compared to internal speeds.

Remote interface can generate a lot of network traffic

Distributed Logic Model

In the remote interface model we separate the user interface component from the rest of the system. What if we partition the business logic itself? We can run these partitions on many computers in the network to take advantage of any special hardware capabilities that match the application function.

Splitting the business logic

For example, we might want to place an inferencing component of a system on a fast RISC-based machine, which is especially well suited for integer arithmetic. On the other hand, we would place the data management component of a system on the machine where the database resides (Figure 10.10).

Example

One way to take advantage of the distributed logic model is by building application servers. Mission-critical distributed *on-line transaction processing* (OLTP) systems in a networked environment commonly use application servers in order to achieve maximum performance.

Application servers use the distributed logic model

Figure 10.10 Distributed logic model

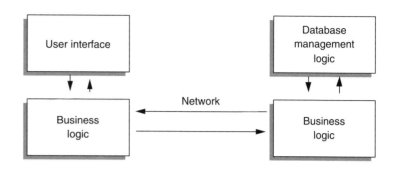

A client component mostly handles the user interface

To build a system which uses the distributed logic model, a programmer would have to write both client and server components. A client component is dedicated to providing the user interface function, and can be written using any language, with a preference given to portable libraries like XVT or Zinc.

The rest lives on a server

A server component contains the business logic code and the data management code. It is best written in traditional languages like C, but can also be written in database-specific languages like Sybase's Transact-SQL.

Commands to the server come from user actions

In a typical exchange, user selection of a window, or a click on a button, results in a message being sent from the client to the server application. These messages are high level "commands," and map directly to some business function that needs to be performed.

Example

For example, a request like "update claim for Jones," will probably result in a series of SQL calls to the database. This series of calls constitutes a *transaction*. A transaction is certainly not limited to the database activity, and can involve calls to image- and knowledge-based servers.

Approach #1: Stored Procedures

Stored procedures are application extensions

There are at least two ways to implement the application servers. One approach is to use a database provided feature called *stored procedures.* You can think of a stored procedure as a subroutine in a programming language. A stored procedure gets invoked in the same way that a subroutine is called within an application. The difference here is that a stored procedure resides on another machine in the network, namely the database server.

Many high end database vendors like Sybase, Oracle, and others implement stored procedures by extending the standard SQL with transaction constructs, variables, control structures (`while..do`, `repeat..until`), etc. For example, in Sybase's Transact-SQL you can declare variables, set up `while` loops, and perform many other "non-SQL" tasks.

Many database vendors offer stored procedures

Stored procedures are precompiled and stored in the database server. The client application invokes a stored procedure, which executes on the server, and the results, if any, are sent back. In a transaction-oriented application, stored procedures can significantly improve performance.

They are stored in a DBMS

Example: SQL Server

Suppose we have a customer order tracking application, and we would like to write a stored procedure that would check to see if the customer is indeed a valid customer of ours and then mark the order as "approved." We have the following two database tables:

Stored procedure example

Customer	Orders
name	cust_name
address	order_num
city	status
address	
zip	

We write the stored procedure as follows:

```
create_proc   check_order
  @customer_name      varchar(30)
as
  if exists ( select name from customer
            where name = @customer_name )
    print" Valid customer"
```

```
          else
            update orders
            set status = "approved"
            where cust_name = @customer_name
```

Example explained

The first line simply declares a stored procedure and names it check_order. Line number two declares a parameter with which check_order will be called, customer_name. The third line validates that the customer record exists in the customer database and that the customer is a valid one. As you have probably noticed, the if..then...else statement is a language construct and extends Transact-SQL beyond SQL. The last three lines update the table of orders to reflect that the customer has been approved.

Very little work is performed at run time

After the stored procedure is compiled, it gets stored in the database. During compilation, the database engine figures out how it will physically access the needed data. This is known as the *execution plan*. When the procedure check_order is called, all the database engine needs to do is to look up the execution plan and execute it.

A stored procedure can be invoked interactively, as follows:

```
execute check_order smith
```

The following simple C code demonstrates how to invoke a stored procedure from an application:

```
int main()
{
  LOGINREC  *login;          /* structire contains user info */
  DBPROCESS *dbproc;         /* structure used to communicate */
                             /* SQL server */
  /* alloc and initialize login struct */
  logon = dblogin();
  DBSETLUSER(logon,"my_id");
  DBSETLPWD(login,"my_passwd");
  DBSETLAPP(login,"app_name");

  /* open the database */
  dbproc = dbopen(login,"dbsrv");

  /* add the command to invoke our stored procedure */
  dbcmd(dbproc,"check_order smith");

  /* send to the server for execution */
  dbsqlexec(dbproc);
}
```

The first few lines establish the user's login context so that a database can be opened. Once the database is opened, the user builds a command buffer and sends it over to the server for execution.

Stored procedure invocation

A word of caution is required: The database-provided languages, like Sybase's Transact-SQL, are proprietary and therefore not portable. If you decide to switch to another database vendor, you will be able to port most of the standard SQL code, but not much else.

Caution!

Approach #2: Using a Transport Protocol and Traditional Programming Languages

Another approach to implementing distributed logic application servers is to separate the logic into client and server components, and to write the necessary communications code that would pass commands and data between them. To write the communications code, you will need to learn how to use a transport protocol like NetBIOS, SPX/IPX, or TCP/IP.

This approach involves network programming

In order to give you some feeling for what is involved, we will look at a simple pair of client/server applications that communicate using the NetBIOS interface. Before we dig into all the gory details of NetBIOS programming, let's look at how the exchange of data and commands takes place, from a bird's eye view.

Distributed application example

The easiest way to explain how computers communicate is to compare it with the way people communicate, specifically, to a telephone conversation. Suppose that a client and server wish to communicate with each other (Figure 10.11). Before two people can talk to each other on the telephone, their telephone numbers must be registered with a telephone company. The analogous task for computers is accomplished by the NetBIOS Add_name command. After its execution, the client and server are "in the yellow pages," so to speak.

NetBIOS sessions are analogous to a telephone conversation

The server indicates that it will answer client calls by executing the NetBIOS command *listen*. Meanwhile, the client dials the server's number by issuing the NetBIOS command *call*.

NetBIOS call command

Figure 10.11 Conversation

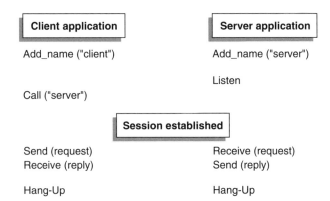

Client application	Server application
Add_name ("client")	Add_name ("server")
	Listen
Call ("server")	

Session established

Send (request)	Receive (request)
Receive (reply)	Send (reply)
Hang-Up	Hang-Up

Conversation

Once the server answers the phone, the two are in session. Being in session allows either party to speak (send data) or to listen (receive data). The client and server terminate their conversation by executing the NetBIOS command *Hang-Up*.

Computer communication resembles human communication

As you can see from this simple example, computer communications are very much modeled after human communications. After all, we have created computers in our own image.

Example: NetBIOS programming

A simple client/server example

Now we will consider the details of NetBIOS programming. This example will assume that both client and server programs are applications executing under DOS. I have purposely kept these programs simple. Here again, my intent is to give you an idea of what is involved in NetBIOS programming and not to make you an expert NetBIOS programmer.

Interrupt 0x5C

First we will consider some basics. All NetBIOS commands can be issued using interrupt 0x5C. In order to execute a NetBIOS command, an application fills in a *network control block* (NCB). Let's first consider a low level function that would submit all NetBIOS commands.

```
void CallNetbios(NCB far *ncb)
{
  struct SREGS sregs;
  union REGS regs;
```

```
    /* first establish addressibility to ncb struct */
    sregs.es = FP_SEG(ncb);
    regs.x.bx = FP_OFF(ncb);
    int86x(0x5C, &regs, &regs);
}
```

This function establishes a pointer to ncb struct and then executes interrupt 0x5C, passing it the address of a NCB. We will use the CallNetbios function from other higher level routines. These functions will become the building blocks upon which our simple client/ server application will be built.

NetBIOS has a single entry point

```
/* this function adds a name to NetBIOS */
char AddName(char *name )
{
  NCB ncb;

  memset(&ncb, 0, sizeof(NCB) );         /* clear out ncb */
  ncb.ncb_command = ADD_NAME_WAIT;        /* load command */
  strcpy(ncb.ncb_name, name);        /* copy application name*/

  CallNetbios(&ncb);                      /* call netbios */
  return(ncb.ncb_retcode);          /* return return code */
}

/* This function is called when a client application */
/* wants to establish a session with a server application */
char CallServer(char *client_name, char *server_name,
                char *lsn)
{
  NCB ncb;

  memset(&ncb, 0, sizeof(NCB) );
  ncb.ncb_command = CALL_WAIT;
  strcpy(ncb.ncb_callname, server_name);   /*set server name*/
  strcpy(ncb.ncb_name, client_name );    /* set client name */

  CallNetbios(&ncb);

  *lsn = ncb.ncb_lsn;       /* return session handle to appl */
  return(ncb.ncb_retcode); }

/* this function is called by the server application */
/* when it is ready to establish a session with the */
/* client application */
char Listen(char *name, char *lsn)
{
  NCB ncb;
```

```c
    memset(&ncb, 0, sizeof(NCB) );
    ncb.ncb_command = LISTEN_WAIT;
    strcpy(ncb.ncb_name, name );            /* set client name */
    strcpy(ncb.ncb_callname,"*");       /* listen to ANY client */

    CallNetbios(&ncb);

    *lsn = ncb.ncb_lsn;        /* return session handle to appl */
    return(ncb.ncb_retcode);
}

/* this function is called to send a message */
char SendMessage(char *message, char lsn )
{
    NCB ncb;                             /* network control block */

    memset(&ncb, 0, sizeof(NCB) );
    ncb.ncb_command = SEND_WAIT;
    ncb.ncb_buffer = message;        /* set pointer to message */
    ncb.ncb_length = strlen(message);        /* set its length */
    ncb.ncb_lsn = lsn;                   /* set session number */

    CallNetbios(&ncb);

    return(ncb.ncb_retcode);
}

/* this function is called to receive a message */
char RecvMessage( char *message, char lsn)
{
    NCB ncb; /* network control block */
    memset(&ncb, 0, sizeof(NCB) );
    ncb.ncb_command = RECV_WAIT;
    ncb.ncb_buffer = message;        /* set pointer to message */
    ncb.ncb_length = 255;                /* size of our buffer */
    ncb.ncb_lsn = lsn;                   /* set session number */

    CallNetbios(&ncb);
    return(ncb.ncb_retcode);
}

/* call thid function to disconnect a session */
char Hang_up(char lsn)
{
    NCB ncb; /* network control block */
    memset(&ncb, 0, sizeof(NCB) );
    ncb.ncb_command = HANGUP_WAIT;
    ncb.ncb_lsn = lsn;                   /* session to diconnect */
```

```
    CallNetbios(&ncb);

    return(ncb.ncb_retcode);
}
```

Our simple client and server code would look as follows:

```
/* client program */

void main()
{
    char rc;                            /* return code */
    char response[256];                 /* communication area */
    char session;                       /* session handle */

    /* add Netbios name */
    if ( ( rc=AddName("client")) == 0 )
    {
        if ( (rc=CallServer("client","server",&session) ) == 0 )
        {
            SendMessage("money, please," session);
            RecvMessage(response, session);
            HangUp(session);
        }
    }
}

/* server program */
void main()
{
    char rc;                            /* return code */
    char request[256];                  /* communications area */
    char session;                       /* session handle */

    if ( ( rc=AddName("server")) == 0 )
    {
        if ( (rc=Listen("server",&session) ) == 0 )
        {
            RecvMessage(request, session);
            SendMessage("ok", session); HangUp(session);
        }
    }
}
```

Our client application announces itself to the world (AddName) and proceeds to connect to the server (Call). Meanwhile, the server has already announced its presence (AddName) and is now ready to receive incoming calls from clients (Listen). Once a session is established,

NetBIOS calls involved in this exchange

DISTRIBUTED LOGIC MODEL

the two applications exchange messages (`SendMessage`/`RecvMessage`) and disconnect (`HangUp`).

Benefits of Using Transport Protocols

There are many benefits to using transport protocols:

- Server applications can be written in C, COBOL, or any other language that supports embedded SQL. These servers are database-independent. If you decide to use another server database, you can easily port the server code to it, because API support for these languages is virtually universal among the database providers.

- There is also more flexibility in the client/server exchange. A client application can carry on a dialog (multiple bidirectional requests) with a server, which is highly desirable for more complex processing. Both applications have control over the number of messages sent and the frequency. Having this control will help build applications that use the network wisely.

- Server applications written in a 3GL can take advantage of threads and processes for better concurrency and higher performance. It is a lot easier to integrate a 3GL server application to other non-SQL sources of information, such as file systems or optical storage devices.

- Our experience shows that the performance of application servers is significantly higher than that of database servers. In some cases, the application servers are twice as fast as the database servers. Sending a series of SQL requests across the network is significantly slower than sending a single request/reply message and performing local SQL calls.

    The primary reason for the slow response of database servers, is that SQL statements are sent to them one at a time. In contrast, an application server eliminates network delay by executing SQL calls directly on the database machine.

- The old rule of mixing CPU-bound and I/O-bound processes still has a place in the distributed world. Since the application server is performing CPU-bound and I/O-bound work, the overall system utilization is more balanced, which contributes to overall higher system performance. Compare this to the remote data management model, where the client does most of the CPU-intensive work and the database server does I/O-bound work. A question that is often asked about the application servers is, "Aren't you shifting the load from the client to the server machine? Won't the server slow down, because it has to process significantly more application code?"

The application code which gets shifted to the back end is common code that can be shared by all client applications, and assuming that it is reentrant, it does not introduce much overhead. For example, our test application server contained most of the business logic and all of the data management code.

In a test we conducted, only 25% of a 486 25-MHz CPU was used to support 40 concurrently active users. A similar test was done using the remote data management model. The results were less encouraging. The client machines were always overloaded in terms of CPU and memory, mostly because the bulk of the applications executed on the client.

We found that 90–95% of system resources were consumed on a client machine (8 Mbytes) resulting in heavy paging and thus degrading performance. The server machine showed some I/O activity, but was hardly taxed at all in terms of CPU utilization (10–15%).

- Another significant advantage of the distributed logic model is that it clearly defines how a system in one department can communicate with another system in another department. As an example, you might want to integrate two separately developed systems in order to present a customer with a single bill.

The separation of the user interface code from the rest of the server code opens up the server for accessibility by other systems. What this means in terms of an enterprise is that a large and complex business function can be delegated to a series of servers. Each server can specialize in performing one or more subtasks. A large task can be accomplished through server-to-server cooperation.

The result is a business system with less code redundancy, clearly defined component architecture that's easier to maintain, and a lot of inherent fault-tolerance. For example if one of the servers is down, then only a part of the system is affected. In a nondistributed system, the entire system becomes unavailable.

Another beneficial side effect of user interface separation is that other methods of interfacing become possible. For example, a fax machine can become a client: when a customer faxes in a request, the server can be triggered to start processing it immediately.

- As already mentioned, the client communicates with the server by sending a high level message containing the name of the transaction to be executed, along with some parameters. This is a form of RPC that results in a single request and a single reply. For most transaction-oriented applications, this form of communication suffices.

- Application servers can be thought of as a set of intelligent objects. I use the word *object* deliberately to emphasize that servers are not just data and code. Servers encapsulate code and data. Each function that a server can perform will either use data or change data.

This combining of code and data is very desirable for several reasons. When a certain set of data is associated with code that manipulates it, the behavior of the system becomes more predictable and easier to understand.

Another benefit is that the internals of how a certain function is performed can be changed without impacting the whole system. This becomes possible, because the knowledge of how a certain function is performed is hidden from the client program, and as long as the server maintains a consistent interface to the client, internal server changes are not disruptive.

Disadvantages of the Distributed Logic Model

Of course, the distributed logic model is not a panacea, and has some weaknesses:

- From a programming point of view this model is more difficult to implement, because in addition to the front end tool, the programmer has to know how to use some sort of peer-to-peer transport protocol like NetBIOS or TCP/IP. In order to build distributed applications quickly, the communications APIs have to be simplified. Many of the difficulties of direct programming to transport protocols can be overcome if a middleware communication product is used. A good middleware product should have a simple programming interface and should hide the complexities and differences of any network.

  Another difficulty is the implementation of an application server. The server has to be able to support tens, and possibly hundreds, of clients concurrently while delivering reasonable performance, assuring data integrity, and remaining very efficient in its utilization of system resources. This requires knowledge of the operating systems' internals, like threads, interprocess communication facilities, memory management, etc.

- If you are building a decision-support type of application, this is probably not the right model. Since transactions are coded in C or COBOL, they are more difficult to change. Remember that transactions are "compiled" to the database. The access plan is formed at compile time, not at run time. If your application creates SQL statements on the fly, or if it has to maintain a set of easily changeable precanned queries, it is probably best to use a decision-support tool, such as Forest & Trees.

The Remote Data Management Model

The remote data management model is achieved by separating the data management code from the rest of the system (Figure 10.12). The data management component is typically a file or a database server that performs data manipulation on behalf of a client

Remote data management is very popular

application. The remote data management model is the most commonly used distributed model today, because of widespread use in commercial products like PowerBuilder SQL Windows.

Remote data management has been around for many years

Remote data management has been well understood for many years. IBM CICS systems have implemented facilities like *function shipping,* which provides basic file redirection services. Using function shipping, a CICS application running on one computer can issue calls to open, read, or write to a file on another CICS system.

Figure 10.12   Remote data management model

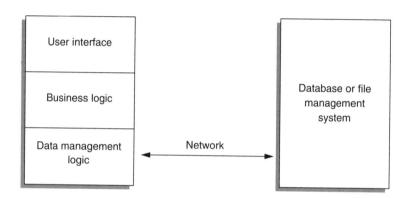

In the UNIX world, distributed file systems have also been around for many years. The function of a distributed file system is to read and write data located in files on other machines in the network. In UNIX terms, a remote file system is mounted on the local machine, enabling such access. In the PC world, remote data management has been implemented in two forms: the file server and the database server. Distributed file systems are an example of remote data management.

Example: A File Server

File servers provide remote drives

File servers play a role very similar to that of distributed file systems. They allow applications and users to access files on remote server machines. Another name for this model is the *redirected drive model.* To access data on another machine using file servers, a programmer builds an application that opens, reads, and writes to a file as if it were local.

A *redirector* makes a remote disk drive appear to be local. This is accomplished by mapping a remote drive to a local drive letter. For example, a program might refer to a file named `k:\customer.dat`, which is physically located on a file server's drive (Figure 10.13).

A remote drive is mapped locally

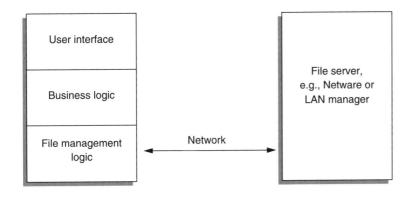

Figure 10.13   File server

File Server Disadvantages

When a client application makes a file I/O request to the operating system or to an index-sequential file manager like Btrieve, the request is intercepted by the I/O redirector and sent across the network to a file server for processing. The file server responds to the user application with a result. This is a very primitive and often inefficient way to build networked applications. For example, when your application makes an I/O request, many data are brought over the network into your client workstation when maybe all you need is just a couple of bytes.

File redirection can create a lot of unnecessary network traffic

This might not seem like a big deal when your application is running on a 16-Mbit token ring network, but if you are considering running this application from home or a hotel room across an asynchronous dial-up line using a modem, you will run into performance problems.

On slow links, the performance will be impacted

Another very important issue to consider is the interoperability of your system with other systems in the company. If another system needs to make requests to your system, do you let them get directly at your data files? Do you make a copy of your data for them? In this model there is no good solution to systems' interconnectivity, because

This model offers poor interoperability

the entire application structure runs on every workstation, and there is no common entry point to which other systems can connect.

Poor use of system resources

Another potential downside to this model is its uneven use of computing resources. Since an entire application is executing on every machine, the machine itself can become a potential memory and processor bottleneck. On the server side, the problem is just the opposite. While the server machine has plenty of CPU cycles to spare, it usually reaches an I/O bottleneck in accessing secondary storage and in LAN adapters.

Advantages

Good for simple applications

Despite its many shortcomings, this model is still very useful for sharing files located on a shared network drive. It is also easy to implement. You can take a stand-alone PC application and make it network and multiuser aware, by taking advantage of the operating system file sharing capability.

Example: A Client/Server Database Server

Client/server database example

This approach has become very popular over the last couple of years, and involves what essentially amounts to decoupling of the database API from a DBMS. The developer typically writes the client component using a 4GL tool like PowerBuilder or SQL Windows. These tools in turn provide high level *links* to one or more off-the-shelf database servers like Sybase, Oracle, or Database Manager (Figure 10.14).

Figure 10.14 Client/server DBMS server

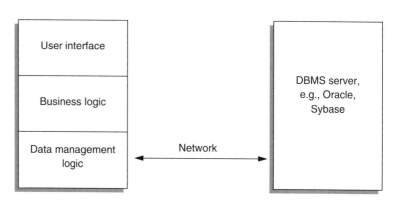

The front end tool communicates with a back end DBMS using the communications software provided by the database vendors. A client application passes SQL statements to the database front end component, which in turn sends them to the database server for processing. The database server processes these requests and returns the results to the client.

SQL requests are sent to a server

Advantages

This approach is more efficient than the file server approach, because it distributes processing more evenly between the client and server machines. The database server accesses the data, sorts them and counts them, before passing the results back to the client. In contrast, a file server would pass all the data back to the client for further processing.

More balanced use of resources

Another advantage to this model is that it generates less network traffic than the file server, because SQL is more declarative, high level, and set oriented. A program using SQL requests a *view* of the data, allowing the server to perform processing (on the server machine) to derive the view. In contrast, requests sent to the file server are basic file read and write requests expressed in terms of physical sectors. As you have probably guessed, returning sectors of a file does not require any server processing.

Less network traffic

Disadvantages

There are some disadvantages to this approach. Just like the file server approach, it suffers from the lack of a clearly defined path for system-to-system interoperability, because the entire application structure (Figure 10.1) is executing in every machine. If another application needs to communicate with this system in real time, how can it connect?

Poor interoperability

As a business system implementor, you are probably concerned about the efficiency of the code that your development tool produces. While one can argue that a high level tool like Gupta's SQLWindows or Powersoft's PowerBuilder makes the programmer more productive, the real issue is whether the performance of the system will be acceptable to the users. One solution might be to use tools like

Poor code efficiency

PowerBuilder for less critical components, and to use C in places where efficiency is needed. Another possible pitfall of using 4GL tools is that the code you write is not portable outside of the tool. If the system is written in C or COBOL, you can always move your code to another platform or choose another compiler vendor.

Limits to application growth

Probably the most overlooked factor in 4GL front end development is that you cannot (realistically speaking) develop a large system that performs well. The code generated by the interpretive 4GL tools tends to run slower, in fact much slower than compiled 3GL code. Our experience shows that 4GL code doing compute-intensive work runs 300–400 % slower than equivalent 3GL code. Also, 4GL applications are very large in size due to their interpretive nature and large run-time support *dynamic link libraries* (DLLs) (often more than 1 Mbyte).

Example

Consider a typical OS/2 system with 8 Mbytes of RAM. After the operating system (3 Mbytes), the network OS software (1.5 MBytes), e-mail (1 MByte), a peer-to-peer protocol like APPC (2.5 MBytes), and the database requester component (1.5 MBytes) are loaded, there is very little memory left for your application, especially if its memory requirements are high. An overcommitted system will result in poor system performance.

The Distributed Database Model

Distributed databases vary in sophistication

When the data management component can transparently request data from multiple databases located on any computer, you have a form of distributed database (Figure 10.15). The term *distributed database* can be very confusing. Let's spend a moment describing the degrees of sophistication of distributed database capabilities. This will also help you separate *marketectures* (architectures that exist only in the minds of marketing representatives) from product capabilities.

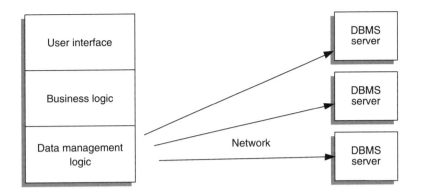

Figure 10.15   Distributed database

The Remote Request

The most elementary form of a distributed database is a remote request. This feature permits the execution of a single SQL request to a single remote database:

Remote Request

```
SELECT SS#, AMOUNT_DUE, DATE_DUE
FROM CUSTOMER
WHERE CUSTOMER# = 123
```

In this simple example we are selecting information from a single table, CUSTOMER. You should note that the remote request is made to a database at one location. Each request constitutes a single transaction. Upon successful completion of the request, the changes to the database are automatically committed, thus making these changes permanent.

Example

Remote requests are easily implemented. The majority of database vendors support remote requests. Remote requests are most appropriate for simple lookup and update operations.

Many database vendors support remote requests

The disadvantage of the remote request is that it allows only a single operation to be performed on a remote database. The database does not maintain an identity with the user application, and therefore sees all incoming requests as atomic and unrelated. Why is that a problem? Well, for a transaction-oriented application, you want be able to roll back (undo) a particular set of operations (a transaction) performed on a database. If the database does not group operations into transactions, it cannot roll them back.

A remote request is inadequate for transaction-oriented applications

The Remote Unit of Work

A remote request takes into consideration transaction boundaries

A more sophisticated form of a distributed database is the remote unit of work. As the name implies, this approach facilitates the execution of a group of SQL statements (a transaction) on a single remote database. The term *unit of work* means that the entire set of SQL statements can be committed or rolled back as a unit (Figure 10.16).

Figure 10.16   Remote unit of work

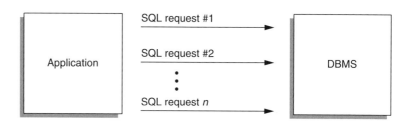

A unit of work can involve updating of multiple tables.

```
BEGIN TRANSACTION

  SELECT AMOUNT_DUE, DATE_DUE
  FROM CUSTOMER
  WHERE CUSTOMER# = 123

  UPDATE CUSTOMER
  SET DATE_DUE = 5/5/94

  UPDATE ACCOUNT
  SET DATE_DUE = 5/5/94

END TRANSACTION
```

Example of the remote unit of work

In this example, the customer table is first updated, followed by updates to the account table. If any of the SQL statements fail, the changes made by all will be backed out. It is also important to note that the requests are still forwarded to a single location.

The Distributed Unit of Work

A distributed unit of work involves more than one database

The next level of sophistication in the distributed database is the *distributed unit of work* (Figure 10.17). In a distributed unit of work, the SQL statements in a single unit of work can address data located at multiple databases. To expand on the earlier example, the customer and account tables could be located on different computers. However, each SQL statement can reference data only at a single computer.

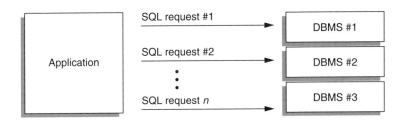

```
BEGIN TRANSACTION

  SELECT AMOUNT_DUE, DATE_DUE
  FROM WASHINGTON.CUSTOMER
  WHERE CUSTOMER# = 123

  UPDATE WASHIGNTON.CUSTOMER
  SET DATE_DUE = 5/5/94

  UPDATE NEW_YORK.ACOUNT
  SET DATE_DUE = 5/5/94

END TRANSACTION
```

The Distributed Request

The most sophisticated form of distributed database technology is the *distributed request* (Figure 10.18). A distributed request removes the limitation of having a single SQL statement address data at a single database. To further expand our example, we can now update databases located at multiple computers with a single SQL statement.

A distributed request can involve more than one remote database request in a single SQL statement

Figure 10.18 Distributed request

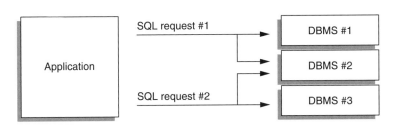

This type of functionality requires highly sophisticated DBMS features:

```
BEGIN TRANSACTION

    SELECT AMOUNT_DUE, DATE_DUE,
    FROM WASHIGTON.CUSTOMER, NEW_YORK.ACCOUNT
    WHERE WASHINGTON.CUSTOMER#=123 AND NEW_YORK.CUSTOMER#=123

    UPDATE WASHINGTON.CUSTOMER, NEW_YORK.CUSTOMER
    SET DATE_DUE = 5/5/94

END TRANSACTION
```

The four models of distributed databases described here are meant to give you a framework for comparing distributed DBMSs. The important point to understand is that the majority of distributed DBMSs today offer only the remote unit of work type of functionality. Some database management systems offer the distributed unit of work feature. A distributed request feature is still years away.

Don't limit yourself to a single model

In this chapter we have examined the various models upon which networked applications are built. Such models represent a base of practical examples from which you can draw on when implementing your system. The most important thing to keep in mind is that no single model represents an absolute choice. Most networked applications make use of at least several of these models, so don't feel constrained!

11

Development Methodology

Chapter 10 introduced you to the most common distributed application models. The aim of this chapter is to build on that information and to identify a process or a set of steps for you to follow in building distributed systems.

Identify a process for building distributed systems

A common name given to a process for building systems is *methodology*. Methodologies are often misunderstood. Some people mistakenly believe that a methodology must be followed verbatim. This gives methodologies a somewhat dogmatic character. In reality, there are many factors outside of any methodology's control that can make or break a project. For example, the quality, dedication, and knowledge of the team's members, the ever-changing business requirements, the availability of funding, and other important factors have just as much impact on the outcome of any project.

Methodologies are only guidelines

The usefulness of any methodology is that it serves as a checklist to help ensure that no important steps have been left out. You can think of a methodology like a cooking recipe. If the steps are closely followed, the chances of making the desired dish are improved. A methodology for building software systems is a set of steps that are based on successfully completed projects. Adhering to it improves a practitioner's ability to successfully complete similar tasks. The goal of every methodology is to capture the knowledge of "what worked well" in order to apply it to subsequent projects.

Methodologies are like the recipes

The set of steps outlined in this chapter should be used in a similar fashion. The author does not pretend to have an all-inclusive set of steps for the analysis, development, and implementation of distributed systems. Instead, the goal is to share with you various techniques that have delivered value and are likely to be of use again.

The goal is to share techniques that have worked in past projects

Proposed Methodology

Object-oriented analysis and design are at the heart of this approach

The proposed methodology makes use of object-oriented analysis and design to create a logical system model. At the same time, a distributed systems model is chosen to serve as a blueprint for this system. The final step of this methodology involves marrying the logical model to a distributed system model. The steps of this approach are as follows:

1 *Create a logical system model*   (a) review user requirements, (b) develop function specification, (c) identify core objects, (d) identify responsibilities and collaborations for each object, (e) identify hierarchical relationships, and (f) animate the model

2 *Select a distributed application model based on*   (a) portability needs, (b) performance needs, (c) implementation time constraints, (d) available tools, (e) technical knowledge, and (f) existing system architecture and legacy systems

3 *Implementation*   (a) logical model transformation, and (b) proof-of-concept implementation

Step 1: Creating a Logical System Model

Today's systems can't keep up with business changes

Today's business systems are often criticized for their inability to keep up with changes in business. By the time a new system is built, it is already functionally obsolete and requires modifications. System changes are never ending. It is becoming clear that systems can no longer be built using existing methods, because existing methods produce systems that are difficult to change and maintain.

Today's systems are too inflexible

The problem with traditional systems building methods such as structured analysis and design is that they are based on a very rigid and sequential process. First, the requirements must be gathered, and only then can analysis and design take place. Living in today's ever-changing world, most people can attest to the following premises:

- The requirements are not always known up front. It is unreasonable to expect the users to hand designers a set of requirements, because their business is constantly changing, and what they need from a system might change in the future.

- System analysis and design techniques must take into account the dimension of time. Structured programming and analysis techniques look only at the requirements as they exist at a point in time. The design of a system must be examined in terms of its durability to withstand system changes, which are inevitable.

Another problem associated with structured analysis and design is that it immediately focuses on *how* a system will perform its operations. That in turn limits the design process to considering only the given set of requirements—very little time is spent anticipating other operations that the system might have to perform in the future.

The traditional approach focuses only on how the system needs to work today

Object-oriented analysis and design (OOA/OOD)

In the last several years, object orientation has become a popular alternative to structured analysis and design. An object-oriented analysis and design initially starts out with a more abstract focus. It focuses on *which* operations the system will need to perform, not *how* they will be performed. Such broader focus creates a system design that is more likely to anticipate and accommodate system changes, because more time is spent in the design phase anticipating system changes. In OOA/OOD, more time is devoted to understanding the business.

OOA/OOD is equally applicable to distributed and stand-alone systems. In fact, an argument can be made that designing distributed system components forces object-like thinking. You can almost think of servers as objects that provide public interfaces.

OOA/OOD is a good fit for distributed applications

OOA/OOD has grown out of a modeling and simulation world. In simulations, a model of something is created to see how to it will change under various conditions. The techniques used to build such models make sure that no operations are *hardcoded* and that new ones can easily be added. One example of such a model would be a stock market simulation. Changes in market conditions are applied to the model in order to predict how the stock market will react to them. Such simulation techniques have always been based on a fundamental

Modeling techniques have always been designed to deal with changes

concept—dealing with change. These simulation techniques have existed for many years, but only in the last decade or so have many people realized the usefulness of modeling techniques to the analysis, design, and implementation of any complex software system.

OOA/OOD focuses on business entities

Unlike structured analysis and design, which focuses on hierarchical function decomposition, OOA/OOD focuses on core business entities. Let's explore this statement in some detail. Hierarchical function decomposition is a top-down technique (Figure 11.1). It begins by taking a required operation and breaking it into subtasks which in turn are decomposed into other subtasks. This process continues until a basic set of modules is defined that makes up a system.

Figure 11.1 Claims management system designed using a hierarchical functional decomposition

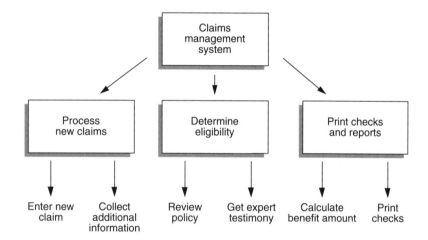

Hierarchical decomposition focuses too much on the current business process

Hierarchical function decomposition looks at a system design from a procedural point of view. It focuses on how the system will perform various tasks. The trouble with this approach is that these same business procedures tend to change a lot. For example, in the insurance business the process by which claims are paid often changes. Core business entities, like claims, are less likely to change. In other words, an insurance company will still continue to deal with claims.

OOA/OOD focuses on the core business entities

Every business has core entities that describe it. In an insurance company, these are claims, insured clients, policies, checks, expert advice, and so on. In a banking business they are checks, loans, deposits, and statements. One logical conclusion might be that systems should be built around these entities and their relationships (Figure 11.2). Consequently, less focus should be placed on how processes are carried out today. Contrary to hierarchical function decomposition, OOA/OOD focuses a system design around the core entities. By placing more emphasis on what the core business entities are and less emphasis on how the system needs to work today, OOA/OOD creates a system model that can better cope with change in the business process.

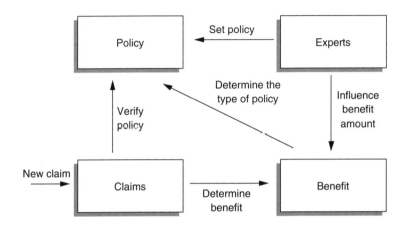

Figure 11.2 Claims management system designed around core business entities

One easy way to find core business entities is to write down a set of noun phrases that describe your business. The initial system design should be focused more around these noun phrases (core business entities) and less around verb phrases (processes).

Core business entities are usually described by noun phrases

Step 1(a): Review user requirements

The first step in system analysis is to review user requirements. User requirements should focus on describing the business problem at hand. Often, the users will try to offer advice on how a task is to be accomplished. A natural temptation is to apply this advice immediately. While users are experts at knowing what they want the system to do, they are not necessarily the best judge of how it should be done. The challenge to a system developer during this phase is to really understand the business problem. This is the right time to clarify any confusing business terminology and to explore at some depth how the business works and how it is likely to change.

Understand user requirements

Step 1(b): Identify core objects

Pick out core business objects

As you read the user requirements, try to pick out core business concepts. From now on let's call them *objects*. I purposely have delayed using this term to give you a feeling for what objects are, without bringing in any preconceived notions. Objects are typically noun phrases that make up a business domain. For example, if we were asked to write an account management system for a bank, chances are that our objects would be things like accounts, bank cards, deposits, withdrawals, personal identification numbers, etc.

Objects embody code and data

Each object embodies both code and data (Figure 11.3). The fancy term for this is *encapsulation* or *information hiding*. The code represents actions that can be done to a particular object, while the data store the state of the object. An object-oriented term for code is *method*.

Figure 11.3   Each object is made up of data, and code that manipulates them

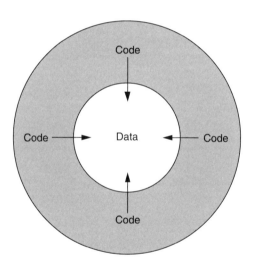

Example

For example, in Figure 11.4 the object account is likely to consist of `updateBalance`, `createAccount`, `deleteAccount`, and other methods (actions) that can be applied to this type of object. The data for an account is likely to consist of the account owner's name and social security number, the current balance, etc.

The work gets done through object collaborations

In an object-oriented system, the work gets done by a collaboration between objects. Think of each object as a specialist in something. When a request to perform a certain function enters a system, possibly through a user action at the keyboard, the objects accomplish the task by communicating with each other. They do so by sending each other messages, which are requests to perform operations, along with some data (arguments).

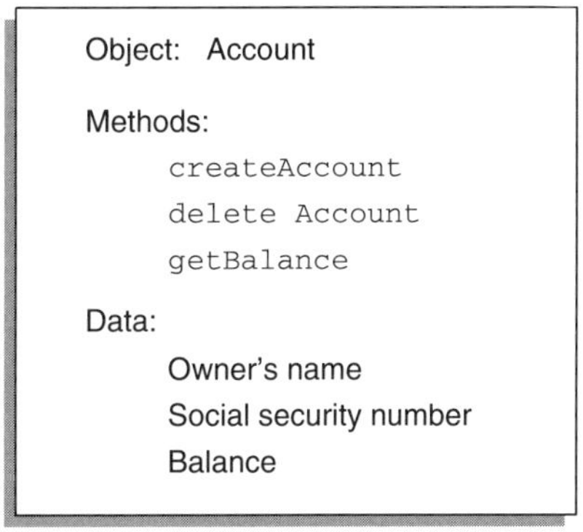

```
Object:  Account

Methods:
        createAccount
        delete Account
        getBalance

Data:
        Owner's name
        Social security number
        Balance
```

Figure 11.4   An object

Getting back to examining user requirements, try to pick out as many objects as you can. At this point, be very generous with your selections, because you can always discard objects that are not needed. Instead of writing object descriptions on a single piece of paper, a better method is to use some 3 × 5 cards. Each card should have the format shown in Figure 11.5. *Internal data* is where you should jot down the object's properties (data). Think of these as internal variables.

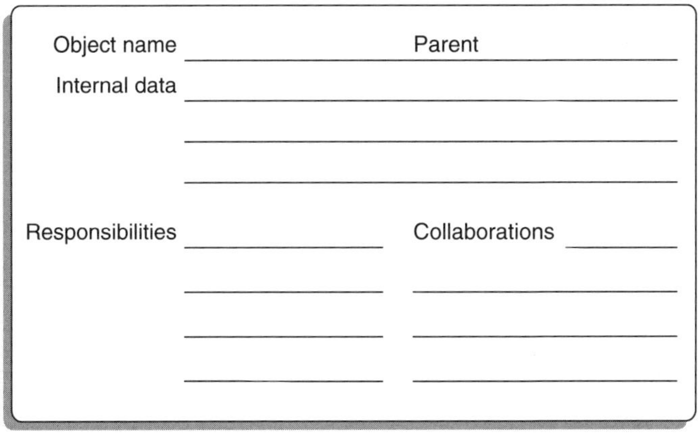

Pick out as many objects as possible

```
Object name _____    Parent _____
   Internal data _____
               _____
               _____

Responsibilities _____   Collaborations _____
               _____                _____
               _____                _____
               _____                _____
```

Figure 11.5   Index card for object description

Step 1(c): Responsibilities and collaborations

An object can perform only its own functions

An object cannot accomplish many tasks on its own. An object can perform only those actions that directly relate to itself. For example, in our banking account management system, an account object should not be responsible for printing transaction receipts.

Each object is responsible for performing its functions

The inevitable question is how any work gets done in an object-based system. The answer is through responsibilities and collaborations. *Responsibilities* are actions that an object has committed itself to performing for all other objects in the system. Once committed, an object cannot remove itself from these responsibilities. For example, a bank account object might commit to the following responsibilities:

- `newAccount` Creates a new account for a customer

- `printAccountStatement` Prints account statement

- `getBalance` Returns the value of the account

- `setBalance` Sets an account's value to the specified amount

- `closeAccount` Closes an account

Often, objects need to collaborate to accomplish user functions

While some responsibilities can be performed entirely by objects on their own, others will require cooperation with other objects. In our banking example, `getBalance` is easily done without any additional cooperation from other objects, but `printAccountStatement` will likely require cooperation from other objects in the system. The object-oriented term for such cooperation is *collaboration*.

At this point you should have a stack of cards with object names identified at the top. Go ahead and try to fill in the internal data, responsibilities, and collaborations for each object. Don't feel compelled to be correct. For now you are simply giving it your best guess.

Step 1(d): Identify hierarchies

Objects often have hierarchical relations to each other

Objects are rarely stand-alone. Typically, some relationship can be found between any two objects. One such relationship is called an *is-a* relationship. This means that one object is a special case of another object. It is a form of specialization and generalization. For example, let's say we have two objects: an automobile and a truck. Each object is distinctly different from the other, but both are a form of transportation vehicle. Put another way, an automobile and a truck have a common parent—a vehicle (Figure 11.6).

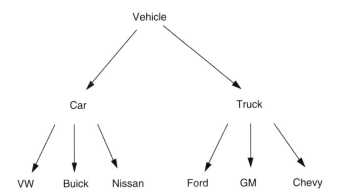

Figure 11.6 Object hierarchy

By identifying such hierarchies, we can define functionality in the parent object that is common to all its children. In our banking example, we might identify a checking and a savings account, but derive a general account object that captures the data and functions that are common to both types of accounts.

Object hierarchies capture common behavior for reuse

There are two reasons for identifying such hierarchies:

- *Code reuse*   If a behavior is common to a group of objects, it is better to capture that code once in the parent object and let its children objects inherit the behavior or data without having to do anything. This can simplify objects.

- *Easier maintenance*   If the code exists only in one place, i.e., in a parent object, any changes to this code need be made only in one place, not in every child object.

Step 1(e): Animate the model

Up to now, we have identified objects that make up our domain, but how can we be sure that we have identified all of them? One very useful exercise is to try to animate the objects at hand. Animation? Absolutely! Simply think of every object as a living thing. After all, each object can respond to messages sent to it, and like most living things, objects store information (data) internally. Thinking of objects this way makes it easier to play out how they cooperate to perform

Animating an object model is an important step in creating well designed systems

operations, and ultimately to design a better system by anticipating how it might be used or how it might change.

Gather function requirements

First, pick out functions from the users' requirements list that the system has to perform. For each function, you need to envision how the various objects will have to collaborate in performing it. In the process, you will likely discover new objects and modify the responsibilities and collaborations of others. For example, our simple bank account management system has to perform the following operations:

1   Open a new account

2   Deposit into an account

3   Withdraw from an account

4   Print an account statement

Our model might look something like Figure 11.7.

Figure 11.7   Object model

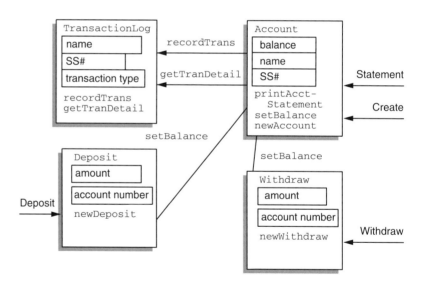

Example object model explained

We have identified four objects: Deposit, Withdraw, Account, and TransactionLog. Each object contains some data (boxed in) and a set of methods. A simple transaction like account creation is handled entirely by an account object. A more involved operation like a deposit takes several objects to accomplish it. First, a deposit object is created that contains the amount to be deposited and the account number. The deposit object sends a `setBalance` message to the account object. The account object adjusts the account balance and sends a `recordTran` message to the `TransactionLog` object, which records transaction details for all accounts. This simple example is meant only to give you some appreciation for OOA/OOD. There is significantly more detail to OOA/OOD, but it is outside of the scope of this book.

This modeling exercise should help you:

- Identify areas of dataflow and control flow in your system, and identify how to structure the system to minimize performance bottlenecks.

- Anticipate how the system will be used and how additional requirements might change the system. But more importantly, you will get a better idea about how to structure the system in such a way that it can better absorb changes.

Step 2: Selecting a Distributed System Model

The next step is to decide which of the models best fits the system requirements at hand. Without a doubt, this is a very difficult process. One way to approach this task is to examine each model and compare it against criteria that are important to your project. Please take a moment to create a list of *guiding principles* for your project. Some of the items on your list should be covered in this section.

Make a list of the guiding principles

Step 2(a): Portability needs

A frequent item on such lists is portability. Portability means being able to easily port your application to another operating systems. For the most part, portability can be achieved in two ways:

Code portability

- By writing a system in an industry standard, portable language that is available from many vendors on many operating systems. These are typically the traditional third generation languages like C, COBOL, or FORTRAN.

- By selecting a tool or a development language that has been ported to run in many environments. A 4GL like SAS, used for statistical analysis is a good example. SAS programs do not need to be modified when they are moved between platforms.

Portability to other environments depends on the development tool

For the most part, portability is determined by the development language or tool, and has less to do with a distributed model; however, a distributed logic model offers more choice. Since application code is separated into front end clients and a back end server, the portability of each component is independent of the other. Using this model, a back end server can be written in a standard language like C, virtually guaranteeing portability to other platforms. The front end can be written using a wide variety of GUI tools and can easily be rewritten, because in the distributed logic model it would contain only the presentation services component.

Step 2(b): Performance needs

Users care about system response time

Only the users of the systems can really determine an acceptable level of performance. Performance criteria need to be set for each function of the system. The users are mostly concerned with a system response time normally measured in seconds. They want to know how long it will take for the system to come back after pressing the enter key.

The performance of a system is determined by many factors

There are many factors that will ultimately determine system performance. The following list highlights the most likely areas in terms of their impact on performance.

- *The network*   To gain maximum performance, a distributed application must take advantage of the processing power available in the network, but at the same time it must use the network with care. A network, especially a wide area network, can easily be flooded with too much data, which will have negative consequences on the performance of many applications. Therefore, there is a strong incentive to select an architecture which minimizes the amount of network traffic.

  Let's examine the behavior of each model in relation to the network. The distributed interface model, which is likely to be a new GUI user interface to a terminal-based system, can change the way this application uses the network. Front ending often entails capturing of multiple screens. Since it is a program and not a person in front of a terminal that responds to terminal screens, the pattern of interaction changes. That in turn can lead to a different pattern of dataflow on the network. That is, the amount of data on the network remains the same, but it tends to spike more frequently.

The remote interface model has a tendency to place a significant load on the network, because it communicates user interface commands and screen changes very frequently. A common complaint about X Window-based systems is their high use of network bandwidth.

The best model, as far as intelligent use of the network goes, can be achieved using the distributed logic model. Using this model, user-written application code has the ultimate control over the amount of data that gets sent on the network, because the communication takes place between application components.

Use of the network by remote data management and distributed database models is determined by the database vendors' implementation decisions. One can only hope that intelligent choices were made.

- *Development tools*   Not all development tools create equally efficient code. Traditionally, compiled languages generate more efficient code than interpretive tools, but interpretive languages are typically faster to develop and debug with. Here a developer needs to make a tradeoff between efficiency of code and development time. To best address stringent performance requirements, a combination of development tools is typically used.

- *Hardware*   Obviously the hardware capacity has a lot to do with any system's performance, CPU speed and and the amount of RAM being at the top of the list. An inadequate amount of RAM will force the system into excessive paging of memory contents in and out to disk, which will reduce the system's performance.

Step 2(c): Implementation time constraint

The amount of time allocated to a project will force you to make many tradeoffs. If a project estimate shows that the project will take a

Tight schedules force compromises

year and a half to complete, and you are only given half a year to implement, something has to give. You can compromise by:

- Reducing the scope of the project. Simply break the project deliverables into a set of smaller, functionally meaningful deliverables. This is often the best way to deal with a time constraint for two reasons. First, business priorities change more quickly today than ever before. If the system's benefits will not quickly become obvious to its users, there is a good chance that the project may get canceled. By breaking a project into a set of deliverables you can significantly improve its chances of survival. Second, reducing the scope of a project often alleviates the need to compromise on tools and architecture that you believe are technically the best fit for the project.

- Choosing an architecture that takes less time to implement. For example, suppose you are asked to replace a large mainframe system that performs the "bread-and-butter" operations of the business, and that you are given four months to accomplish this task. Four months is obviously not enough time to rewrite such a system. Maybe the first step that can be taken in this time is to make use of the distributed interface model and add a GUI front end to an existing system.

- Another option might be not to write the system internally, but to purchase it from a vendor.

Step 2(d): Available tools

Available tools often determine the client/server model

The choice of a distributed system model often gets determined by availability of tools. For example, there are many tools in the marketplace today that support building applications using the remote data management model. SQLWindows, PowerBuilder, and Uniface are some of the most popular tools in this category. At the same time, you might find that very few tools exist to support the distributed logic model, but that will change within the next year or two.

Step 2(e): Technical knowledge

Another consideration that will play a major role in your decision of which distributed model to use is the base of technical skills in your organization. Some companies do not have in-house technical expertise and are more likely to go with a packaged solution or to select a tool with which their staff can learn to program. Other companies, especially more technically oriented ones, are more likely to base their choice on what they perceive to be the right technical solution. Let's review the five models of distributed systems in terms of the skills and knowledge required to implement them.

The technical depth and experience of your staff will play an important role in selecting a client/server model

The distributed interface model can be approached from several directions. The more technically inclined audience might consider programming directly to the EHLLAPI interface, which is normally done in C or COBOL. Others can implement applications using high level and easy-to-program tools like FlashPoint or Easel.

The distributed interface model can be implemented with high and low level tools...

If you are in a shop which predominantly uses UNIX, you are more likely to take advantage of the distributed interface model by using X Window-based technology. This can be done by programming in C or using a 4GL that simplifies X Window programming.

...and with X Window

The most challenging model to implement today is the distributed logic model. The primary reason for this is the lack of tools that simplify the development process. Anyone implementing this model must be savvy in systems and network programming. Given the many benefits of this approach, it is only a matter of time before many tools appear that will simplify development.

The distributed logic model today requires good technical expertise

The most popular distributed model today is remote data management. I believe that this is due to the following reasons. First, there is literally an overabundance of tools that make this model fairly easy to implement from a programming perspective. Second, there is a tendency to "follow the crowd," and so many project teams would not even consider other models because "everyone we know is doing it this way."

The remote data management model is the most popular today

The distributed database model shares many implementation challenges with the distributed logic model. Today, this model requires the developer to take care of many low level details, such as a two-

The distributed database model will gain in popularity

phase commit. This model will become more popular as more and more database vendors offer distributed database features built into their products.

Step 2(f): Existing system architecture and legacy systems

Existing technology will influence your decision on a client/server model

Another major factor in distributed model selection will be based on the technology your shop already has. For example, if there is no mainframe system in your company, than you are not likely to use a distributed interface model. If you are in a predominantly UNIX shop, you are more likely to make use of the remote interface model. The legacy systems will play an important role in your selection process. For example, if a company has built its systems on a CICS platform, more than likely it will look for tools that enable easy and reliable communication between LAN-based systems and the existing CICS systems.

Step 3: Transforming the Logical Model to Implementation

The third and final step of this methodology is to decide how the object model should be implemented. The goal of this step is to prove the technical feasibility of the proposed solution.

Step 3(a): Logical model transformation

An object-oriented tool would offer a one-to-one mapping

In order to transform a logical model of the system, we must make a decision about how to physically implement it. If the chosen development tool fully supports encapsulation, inheritance, and polymorphism, there is a direct mapping from the model to the implementation language.

A nonobject-oriented tool can also be used

If the selected development tool does not support these object-oriented concepts, the transformation is a little bit more challenging, but certainly not impossible. Let's examine some of the techniques which can help in this process.

Use user-defined data types to simulate objects

The basic question is how to implement the notion of an object when it is not supported by your programming language. An object is an encapsulation of both data and code. Structured programming languages like Pascal typically support user-defined data structures. In Pascal they are called *records*. A record contains a collection of built-in or derived data types, and can be thought of as containing instance (an object's internal) variables. Access to these variable should be provided only through a set of procedures and functions. Using this technique, encapsulation can be easily accomplished.

In languages that don't support functions or procedures, e.g., COBOL, an entire module should be treated as an object. In fact object-oriented extensions to COBOL make use of this concept.

Sometimes the entire module must be used

Polymorphic behavior is a little bit more challenging to implement in languages that do not support variable argument function calls. One compromise might have to involve naming methods (functions) based on the type of object to which they belong, and having the function name specify the type of parameter expected.

Polymorphism is more difficult to simulate in nonobject-oriented languages

Object-oriented message passing can be implemented simply as a function, procedure, or a program call. In fact, the majority of object-oriented languages mask message passing via a function call.

Function calls simulate messaging

Implementation of inheritance in a nonobject-oriented language is significantly more challenging. The first requirement is to be able to extend the syntax of the language in order to express subclassing relationship. One way that this can be accomplished is through a language preprocessor like the one found in C. The more challenging task involves writing a control *dispatcher* that transfers control among objects. This task requires a lot of technical skills and should be implemented only if absolutely necessary.

Simulating inheritance in a nonobject-oriented requires some technical challenges

Step 3(b): Proof-of-concept implementation

No matter how confident we are about a design, the only way that designs prove themselves is through implementation. Implementation does not necessarily need to entail the entire system. One easy way to prove the feasibility of the system is to select what is perceived to be the most technically challenging component of the system and implement it first.

Implement one component

In the process, you will likely discover many areas that need redesign or fine tuning. The challenge is to set aside an adequate amount of time to work through the various system glitches.

Set aside time to work out the glitches

A pilot project must be as real as possible

A common trap that many implementors fall into with a proof-of-concept implementation is not treating it as a full blown system. Remember that the proof-of-concept is only a reduction in scope. It must be tested under the same condition as the final system. For example, running a proof-of-concept on only several machines proves very little if the system will be used by 50 users simultaneously in production.

Suggested Reading

G. Entsminger, *The Tao of Objects,* Redwood City, CA: M&T Books, 1990.

R. Wirfs-Brock, Wilkerson, and Wiener, *Designing Object-Oriented Software,* Englewood Cliffs: Prentice Hall, 1990.

M. Rumbaugh, Blaha, Premerlani, Eddy, and Lorensen, *Object Oriented Modeling and Design,* Englewood Cliffs: Prentice Hall, 1991.

G. Booch, *Object Oriented Design with Applications,* Redwood City, CA: Benjamin Cummings Publishing, 1991.

T. Reenskaug, *Working with Objects,* Greenwich, CT: Manning, 1995.

12

Testing

A well-tested application can make the difference between a well-accepted system and a total failure. Look at it from the users' perspective. Users tend to form their opinions based on their first encounters with a system. This is only human! As with other things in life, first impressions are hard to change.

Cost of Quality

In addition to pleasing your users, catching problems during development and testing will also save your company real money. The most fundamental principle in the cost of quality theory states that the earlier a particular problem is found, the less it will cost to fix it (Figure 12.1). As a general guideline, consider the following set of numbers. If it normally costs $10 to fix a problem during system design, the same problem would cost $100 to fix during development, and if caught in production the very same bug could cost as much as $1,000.

The sooner problems are found, the less they cost to repair

The cost of quality (or lack thereof) is even more dramatic in client/server systems. Let's examine one example to help us put these numbers in perspective.

This is even more true in client/server applications

Assume that a problem is discovered in a design review meeting as the team members go through various details of a newly proposed application. The total cost to fix this particular problem can be quantified in terms of the amount of time it takes the group to come up with an alternative solution.

Problems found at design reviews are easy to correct

The same problem becomes more expensive to fix when it is found during testing. It is possible that a tester will experience this problem during a system test and report it to the developers. The total cost of the bug in this case is comprised of the time it takes the tester to

More effort is spent on finding bugs in a system test

narrow down the problem to a set of reproducible steps, plus the time it takes a developer to make code changes, plus the time necessary to rerun all regression tests.

Figure 12.1   Cost of quality

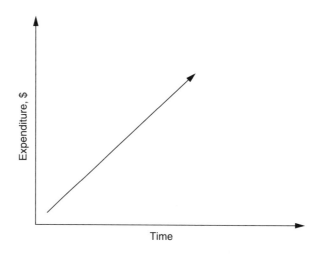

Bugs found in production are very expensive to resolve

What if the problem remains undetected until the system goes into production? The total cost to fix it then includes the cost of system downtime, and can be measured in terms of salaries paid to idle employees, support personnel involved, and revenue lost to the business.

Application problems found in production take a significant amount of time and effort to reproduce and to fix for a number of reasons:

- It is difficult to collect data about exactly what happened. What were the exact steps that led up to the problem? How did it occur?

- What if the users are located in another city? Do you have the tools that would give you remote control over a user's machine? Are there technicians there that can at least apply code changes?

- If you are manually distributing software, think about the effort it will take to update program files on possibly hundreds or thousands of machines! Needless to say, thorough testing must be a top priority.

Testing Client/Server Applications

Testing client/server applications is more challenging than testing a traditional, centralized application. There are a couple of reasons for this. First of all, client/server applications add another variable—the network. The network can be a source of many problems, which can range from wiring failures, to software configuration, to data capacity.

The network adds an element of complexity…

Second, a client/server application is likely to use a graphical user interface (GUI). While there is very little doubt that GUIs are easier to use, they present an incredible testing challenge. A GUI interface gives users many more options for navigating the system. A user is not constrained by a narrow set of menu choices, or a set of function keys at the bottom of the screen. He or she can easily switch between windows, and utilize a wide range of selection options. That translates into additional combinations of paths through the system that need to be tested. In fact, to adequately test a large scale GUI application without automation of testing is next to impossible. We will address the matter of how to automate testing later in the chapter.

…so does a GUI

Start Testing Early

Testing of a client/server application should be an ongoing effort that begins very early in the development process. There are many good reasons to start testing early. For one thing, usability problems can be detected and resolved early, reducing the overall system development time.

Early testing will surface usability issues…

Second, if there are inherent performance problems in your application's technical architecture, you will be able to discover them before much *throw away* code is written.

…and performance problems

And finally, early testing will enable you to break up the system delivery schedule into a set of smaller deliverables, allowing the users to get at least some of the application functions earlier. This piecemeal approach to application delivery will ensure that the system is easy to use and addresses the needs of its users.

Early testing will enable a multiphase approach

The Model Office

The model office *is an excellent intermediate step from development to production*

Many companies that have successfully built client/server applications made use of the model office concept. A model office is an area where the users of a system apply the prototype to do their real work. This has the advantage of putting an application in a real production environment, with minimum impact on the business. There is no better way to uncover additional requirements, assess performance, and receive usability suggestions about the system.

Keep it simple and realistic

A model office does not have to be elaborate or expensive. A simple set up with a couple of machines can suffice for a small project. What is more important is to simulate the users' environment in terms of location, noise level, telephone system, etc.

Example of how not to do it

A few years ago I was involved in a project that did just the opposite. They moved the users from their regular location to newly leased space in another building. This new building was sparsely populated. The noise level was significantly lower, and the phones didn't ring as much. In that environment, the users seemed to be perfectly happy with how the user interface of the system functioned. It was not until the first production release of the system that we discovered that the interface was totally inadequate for the users' environment.

Understand the users' environment

For example, a user would typically handle several customer calls at once and therefore wanted the system to maintain multiple user sessions. Unfortunately, the system was designed for handling calls in a serial fashion. The moral of the story is—make sure you really understand your users' environment.

User rotation is often positive

In order to continue receiving new ideas and suggestions, try rotating as many users as possible through the model office, especially if the users of this system perform different functions. If, for example, you are building an asset management system, the needs of users in the accounting department will likely differ from those in the corporate finance department.

It also helps with training

User rotation gets your users involved. If their suggestions are heard, it helps them develop a sense of ownership of the system. And by the way, you will have gotten a head start on user training!

When selecting a site for a model office, try to locate it as close to the regular user site as possible, in order to simulate the users' typical environment. To minimize disturbances to the development team, create a rotating schedule for the team members to be available to answer user questions and to document feedback. To many developers, seeing users actually use their system to do real work is gratifying. It can also be a real eye-opener. I have seen many programmers truly mystified as to why users couldn't figure out their application's interface.

Make the model office environment as real as possible

Usability Testing

A perfectly functioning system without any bugs can fail miserably if it is not user-friendly. That is precisely the reason for conducting a usability exercise. The goal of a usability test is to measure the effectiveness of the application's interface and ease of navigation. Does the system require a lot of user training? Can a user figure out, with little or no help, how to use it? Can the most common tasks be accomplished easily? Answering such questions will help you measure the usability of your system.

Usability plays a major role in system acceptance and success

Common GUI Design Mistakes

There are a few places where novice GUI designers often make mistakes. The first one is trying to cram too much information into a single screen. Novice interface designers mistakenly think that the more information on the screen, the better the interface. This outdated text-based approach to GUI design produces horrific results. The key to GUI design is to present the right amount of information at the right time.

Don't overcrowd windows with information

Another common mistake is to rely solely on text for the presentation of information, without making good use of graphics and color. If the system you are trying to build uses only textual information, why pay for the extra hardware necessary to run a GUI? The only way to justify a GUI is to make use of its ability to display graphics, text, and color. You should try to represent visually the everyday objects with which the user comes into contact.

Make extensive use of graphics

A comparison between two functionally identical systems

At a recent industry show I attended, a vendor demonstrated its product by showing a side-by-side comparison of a well-designed GUI application and a functionally equivalent text-based system. The application demonstrated was an airline reservation system, and the task being performed was a seat assignment for a passenger. The text-based system would prompt the user with questions like:

- Number of passengers?

- Smoking or nonsmoking?

- Passenger names?

A more visual approach was used

The very same task was then demonstrated using the GUI version. It displayed the seating information visually as a collection of squares (Figure 12.2). The filled-in squares represented the seats that were already taken, and the empty squares represented available seats. Blue was used to show the nonsmoking seats, and red represented the smoking section. A user would make a seat assignment by clicking the mouse on one or more empty seats, at which point the system displayed any information it had about expected passengers. Which reservation system would you rather use?

Figure 12.2 Airplane seating chart

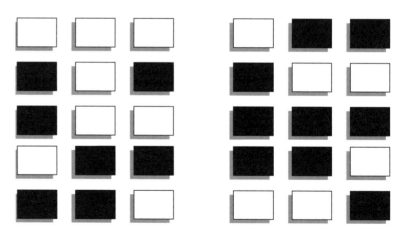

Pictures are often more effective than words

What this and other GUI examples demonstrate is that it is easier for people to interact with and remember images and pictures than text. Studies of the human brain have time and again confirmed these findings.

Creating an easy-to-use system is not so difficult. It takes a little bit of imagination and careful attention to users' needs. A common technique in GUI design is to substitute text with pictures (icons or bitmaps) of easily recognized objects. As the old saying goes, "A picture is worth a thousand words."

A picture is worth a thousand words

A word of caution—whatever metaphor you are using, make sure that it is intuitive. The users should not have to wonder what the picture is trying to convey. If the picture alone does not relate the message, add some text to it. We can learn from Egyptian hieroglyphs. I suspect that there must have been a reason why the Egyptians gave up on icons thousands of years ago!

Add text to pictures if necessary

Usability Labs

A great user interface cannot be designed without user participation. Only when the users really put the interface to work, will you discover how the interface needs to work. Designing a good user interface is an evolutionary process, and therefore requires time to produce a mature product.

User participation in refining the interface is absolutely critical

Most major software development companies now have formal usability labs. A usability lab is a facility where a system is tested for its user-friendliness in a controlled, measured environment staffed by people who are trained to interpret user reactions (usually psychologists).

Software companies have had usability labs for many years

IBM, for example, offers its lab as a service to its clients (for a fee.) A typical usability lab is divided into two sections: one for observers and another for the observed (end user). Through the use of a video camera and other recording equipment, a user is observed performing various tasks with a given application. A review follows to determine which screen elements need improvement.

User actions are recorded and analyzed

Conducting a 1–2 week usability test in a professional usability lab can cost as much as $20,000 to $30,000. If your budget is tight, it is still possible to do a high-quality usability exercise. Here are some tips to help you achieve very professional results.

A usability exercise does not have to be expensive

Set up the Environment

Choose a quiet room

First, set up a quiet room with adequate lighting and divide it into two sections. The user's section should have as few distractions as possible, and merely contain a desk and a computer. The observer's side should be positioned in such a way that all of the user's actions are visible.

If possible, use two video cameras

It is best to conduct a usability test using two video cameras. Point the first camera directly at the screen in order to record all of the user's actions, and point the second camera directly at the user to record his or her facial expressions, body language, etc.

Creating Test Cases

Make the test cases challenging...

The second and probably the most challenging task in usability testing is creating test cases. A test case consists of requests that a user is to perform with an application. Some examples may include adding a new customer to the system, opening a new claim, etc. Please note— the steps specified in a test case should be at the functional level. A common mistake is to include directions on what keys to press and where to click—that is precisely what you want the user to figure out.

...and realistic

Above all, test cases must be realistic. Performing random actions or unrealistic functions on the system does not yield practical results. How do you know if your test cases are realistic? One way to find out is to observe the users' environment and how they interact with a current application (if one exists). Another is to simply ask them. They are the best judges in this matter.

Conducting the Test

Achieve balance in the test group

Find a group of users that is representative of the user community. Make sure that the group is balanced in terms of users with and without computer skills, business functions, and business experience. This will help ensure that your findings are accurate and universal.

Ask the users to verbalize their thinking

When conducting the test, ask each user to announce the task that he or she is about to perform and how it will be performed. Have the user think out loud so that you can capture all of the reasoning process. This will help you isolate places in the interface that the users find difficult to follow. If many users are having trouble in a particular spot, it may be a sign that the interface component needs redesigning.

After each user session, it is helpful to review both tapes at least several times. Many subtle details that are easily missed will come into view. You will be amazed how much an exercise like this can reveal about the usability of a system!

Go over the recording several times

Regression Testing

In addition to being easy to use, a quality system should deliver consistent, error-free behavior. While it is mathematically impossible to prove that a system is free of bugs (and many have tried), consistent and constant exercising of typical user paths through the system can help you to discover problems and thus improve the system's reliability. As its name implies, *regression testing* involves regressing or repeating a series of predefined operations on a system. Continuously regressing can bring out many hidden problems, such as memory leaks, performance bottlenecks, and phantom communication problems.

Continuous regression testing will help eliminate problems

Regression testing is needed especially for client/server applications. Since client/server applications are developed iteratively, they are constantly in a state of flux as a result of code changes, network changes, development tool revisions, and so on. If any of these changes results in new bugs, a well-designed regression test will help you detect and isolate the source of the problems.

Iterative development necessitates regression testing

It is important to keep the steps of regression tests fixed. If the steps are kept constant, finding and resolving bugs in an application is simplified, because the steps that have led to the problem are known. Being able to consistently reproduce a problem in a client/server application is the first crucial step to problem resolution.

Regression testing steps must be held constant

Automated Testing Tools

Continuous regression testing can quickly become very expensive, especially if the system needs constant testing. To reduce the cost of testing and the number of testers needed, companies have successfully applied automated testing tools.

Automated testing tools save time and money

Automated testing tools are ideal for regression testing	An automated test tool is a perfect fit for regression testing, because it can deliver results more consistency than a human tester. Furthermore, regression testing of a large scale system consisting of hundreds of screens is nearly impossible without such a tool.
SQA:Robot example	Let's examine how automated testing tools work by exploring one such tool, SQA:Robot, written by Software Quality Automation.

Example: SQA:Robot

A script file captures user actions	SQA:Robot records all users keystrokes and mouse movements in what is called a script file. A script file is essentially a set of commands that when played back by the automation tool recreates a user's actions. Here is an example of a simple script:

```
$winposref { 0002, 5, 5, 100, 200, ,"demo"
$mm { 10, 20} {000:00:010 }
$mm { 20, 30} {000:00:030 }
{Alt_d}fo
$mb1_d { 300, 300}
```

Script file contents explained	The first line of the script records the coordinate position of a window. It contains information such as the size of the window, its name, movement if any, etc. The second and third lines indicate that a mouse movement took place. The mouse cursor initially was located at coordinates $x = 10$ and $y = 20$. The set of digits to the right is a timestamp, represented as minutes:seconds:milliseconds. The fourth line indicates that the Alt key has been pressed and that letters *f* and *o* followed. A dialog box probably was displayed, and the last line indicates that a left mouse button was clicked. This was likely the result of an item selection in the dialog box or a field positioning within an entry field.
Some commands are added manually	This example is not meant to demonstrate all the features of SQA:Robot, but merely to give the reader an idea of how a typical script might look. Once a script is recorded it can be edited in much the same way as a text file or a program listing. Why would you want to edit a script? The most common reason is to add commands that cannot normally be recorded. For example, one useful feature of many tools is the screen comparison capability. A tester takes a *snapshot* of a portion of a particular screen or the entire screen and saves it out to a file.

When a script is edited, a tester can add a command to compare the screen as it exists during the script's execution to the snapshot previously written to a file. This is commonly done to check for the correctness of a program; i.e., if the two screens or windows compare identically, then the program is performing correctly. Effectively, this feature substitutes having a human tester visually inspect the screens. If the screens are found to be different, the tester can proceed with the script, switch to another script, or quit altogether.

Scripts can compare screens and windows

SQA:Robot saves screen-comparison information to a file. If a particular screen comparison fails, that image is stored in a file with the extension .FAL for further analysis. A tool called *SQA:Robot analyzer* can read the images in a .FAL file and help the user figure out how the captured image differed from the screen image during playback.

Failed screen comparisons are noted

A very useful feature of SQA:Robot is called a *wait state*. Wait states suspend the playback of a script until a certain condition defined by the user is met. There are three types of wait states that can be defined—region compare wait states, window focus wait states, and dialog item wait states:

Wait states help control the timing

- A region compare wait state compares a previously saved image of a screen region with the screen image during playback. SQA:Robot will make a number of attempts (comparisons), before a successful comparison is made or a timeout occurs. The interval for retrying comparisons and the timeout period are set by the user.

- A wait state can also be used to wait until a certain window comes into focus. SQA:Robot will pause the execution of a script until the specified window appears. Here again, timeout and interval retry times can be set by the user. Once a window comes into focus, it can be resized, moved, or given focus.

- Finally, a wait can be defined for a particular item to appear in a dialog box. Once it does, it can be selected (double-clicked), changed, etc.

All three wait states give the tester more control and flexibility during script execution.

Stress Testing

Stress testing focuses on the boundary conditions

How can you be confident that a system will adequately perform even during peak usage? The answer is by performing *stress testing*. As the name implies, stress testing should push the system to its limits to be sure that every boundary condition has been identified and successfully tested.

A stress test must be realistic

Stress testing requires a lot of creative thinking on the part of the tester. Simply brutalizing a system with a set of unrealistic tests will not produce accurate peak usage results. Thus, a stress test first and foremost must be realistic.

Identify all boundary conditions

Start by putting together a well thought-out plan. First the plan should identify all possible boundary conditions that could cause application problems. A possible list would include:

- Running out of buffer space in a database

- A low memory condition in a server causing significant paging

- Running out of disk space for a swapper file or other storage needs

- Reaching high database contention

- Exceeding the number of communication sessions in a transport protocol

- Reaching the maximum allowed number of concurrent users

Common ways to simulate problems

After a list is created, give some thought to whether each condition is realistic. If a condition is indeed realistic, then try to create it and see how the application behaves. There are many simple ways to simulate problems. The table below lists some common problems and ways to simulate them.

Condition	To simulate
Running out of buffer space in a database	1 Configure the buffer space artificially low
	2 Simulate a very large number of users with an automated testing tool
Low memory condition in a server machine	1 Write a simple program that allocates a specified amount of memory from the operating system. Microsoft ships a stress application with their C compiler that can also be used.
	2 Set the pagable/swappable area on disk to an artificially low number. In Windows, this can be accomplished through control application in the 386 enhanced section. In OS/2 it can be set in the SWAPPER statement of CONFIG.SYS.
Running out of disk space for a swapper file or other storage needs	1 Write a program that creates a large garbage file, forcing your application to get a file creation/file write error
	2 Control the size of the swapper file as described above

Condition	To simulate
Reaching a high level of contention in a database	1 If you have a large number of workstations, use an automated testing tool to simulate a large number of users. Most automated tools will allow you to control the rate at which scripts are played back. Set it as high as possible.
	2 Figure out how your application locks database pages during execution. Write an application that "grabs" these pages before your application tries to access them.
Exceeding the number of communication sessions allotted to your application	1 Decrease the number of sessions available per machine
	2 Allocate extra sessions to force the condition
Reaching maximum concurrent users	1 The best way to do this is by using an automated testing tool. Certainly, you can also work with live users.

Keep accurate records

As you simulate various conditions, keep a good record of the system's behavior. This information should be summarized in an easy-to-reference notebook and given to an application support group. It will help the group's members trouble-shoot problems in production, if they can recognize their symptoms.

All test cycles must run at least several times

There are a number of important factors that should influence your stress testing approach. One of them is duration. How long should a particular script run? While there are no hard and fast rules, a minimum of 24 to 48 hours is reasonable. If a system can return a consistent set of results after running for 24 to 48 hours, you can feel reasonably confident about its behavior. In deciding how long to run a particular script, focus first on duration of its test cycles. How many test cycles are there and how long does each take? Whatever the answer, be sure that the amount of time allotted for a script test would allow every test cycle to run at least several times.

Another important factor to take into consideration is the rate or intensity of users' requests. In a given period of time—let's say an hour—how many transactions does a user execute? Usage intensity varies widely. Some users spend most of their time on the phone or away from their desks, only occasionally using systems. Their systems usage resembles an interrupt driven computer. Others, especially in data entry, are *heads-down* users.

The rate of request is another important variable

If a system under development will be a replacement for an existing system, one can learn a lot from examining how the existing system is being used. Pay particular attention to the average number of users per day or per hour. What is the nature of their interactions with the system? What are the peak hours of usage?

A lot of useful information can be obtained from a legacy system

Performance Testing

Performance testing should focus on measuring the average response times for various functions of a system and ensuring that they meet user expectations. Being "systems people," we often get carried away with technical metrics measured in bits per second, utilization percentages, etc. We forget that what our users care about has very little to do with these numbers. Our users want to know how long they will have to wait for the system to respond. Users describe performance requirements in terms of a system's response time. You probably will be asked questions like, "What is the response time of the system for 80% of the tasks?"

When it comes to system performance, the users care about response time

To be able to intelligently answer such questions, performance testing needs to be started in the early stages of system development and should remain an ongoing task. Another reason behind the early start goes back to the cost of quality, which states that early problem

Start performance testing early

detection and correction is the least expensive. If the architecture that you had in mind will not deliver desired performance results, catching it early will give you adequate time to react!

Performance problems are real problems

Among the various kinds of testing, performance testing somehow gets ignored or postponed. The usual excuses given go something like, "Oh, we can always tune it later," or, "We are so busy fixing real problems that we don't have the time now." All of us have said these things from time to time, but we were dead wrong. From a user's perspective, a slow system is just as irritating as a system with bugs. Performance problems are real problems!

Mechanics of Performance Testing

Response time, through-put, and utilization

The performance of a system is commonly measured in terms of three widely used metrics: response time, throughput, and utilization. An ongoing performance test should keep track of all three metrics.

- *Response time*   This metric simply measures the time between a user making a request (selection or enter keystroke) and receiving an answer. From a user's perspective, this is the most important metric, because it directly relates to his or her perception of a system's responsiveness.

- *Throughput*   Throughput is a measurement of user-defined units of work for a given period of time. For example, we may say that a certain database delivers 20 transactions per second or that a network has a 4-Mbit-per-second throughput.

- *Utilization*   Utilization is a measure of how busy a certain resource is. It is directly proportional to the rate of requests sent to a resource. Utilization is expressed in terms of the percentage of time that a resource is busy processing requests.

Metrics alone are insufficient

Metrics are merely numbers, and by themselves cannot explain changes in a system's behavior. To be able to determine what causes changes in performance, one must understand some of the major factors that impact it. Let's examine these factors.

Network

Too often, the network gets blamed for an application's poor performance, and often undeservingly so. If the speed of the network really is a problem for a given application, it will become very apparent early in the testing. If a network-related performance problem materializes in the later stages of testing, it is often caused by factors outside of the application. Some causes could be:

- Increases in the network traffic as result of newly added users

- Changes in the network topology resulting in congestion in bridges or routers

- Malfunctioning (streaming) network adapters causing excessive soft errors which result in retransmissions of data

- Ineffective tuning of message and buffer sizes

- Exceeding network operating resources such as buffers, sessions, or link stations

Network problems can usually be identified in the early stages of testing

Application architecture

If an application makes poor use of network resources, it will become very apparent in the early stages of performance testing. For example, if you build a Dbase application that uses a large database file stored on a network drive, and the application is used by a large group of people, there is a good chance that its performance will be unacceptable, because of the large amounts of data sent through the network.

Poor architectural decisions should become apparent early in testing

I was once asked to look at a client/server GUI application that took over 30 seconds to respond after the first *OK* button was clicked. Looking closely at the system, I noticed that every entry field in the current window was associated with a stored procedure in the database server. Stored procedures performed syntactic and semantic field validation. Crossing the network for every field validation was a clearly inappropriate use of the network.

Example of what not to do

Number of concurrent users

Place the emphasis on the word *concurrent*. As an example, consider a customer support application and a data-entry application. A customer support representative spends quite a bit of time on the phone,

Simulate the maximum concurrent number of users

and system usage is occasional. A clerk entering enrollment information is constantly exercising the system. Both applications may have the same number of users, but they don't have the same number of *concurrent* users. Make sure that the maximum number of concurrent users is known, and try to simulate how they use the system.

Available memory in client and server machines

Lack of available memory will cause excessive paging and impact performance

Having sufficient memory to run is always an important requirement for any application. In the client/server application world, having a sufficient amount of memory takes on additional importance. Consider a Windows or OS/2 application that is served from a network drive. Such an application is made up of segments. When a user starts the system the segments are loaded across the network into a workstation's memory. If the amount of memory in the workstation is insufficient, application segments will quickly get discarded. When a discarded segment is needed again, another network trip will be necessary. Such constant discarding and reloading of segments will negatively affect performance!

Performance degradation can be observed through key metrics

A server machine with an inadequate amount of memory will resort to excessive paging, thus degrading performance. This condition is relatively easy to spot, because it is characterized by an unusually sharp drop in response time as the number of users increases. The same information can also be observed by the drop in throughput and a jump in server utilization.

Database tuning

Memory often equals performance

The configuration parameters of a database engine can have a significant impact on an application's performance. One such parameter is typically known as a *buffer pool*. A buffer pool controls how much data is kept in memory rather than left on the secondary storage. A server machine might have a lot of available memory, but if the buffer pool is not set up to take advantage of it, the performance will suffer. A general comment that can be made for all client/server databases is that memory equals performance.

Now that you are familiar with the factors that impact performance, put together a plan that monitors such factors. For example, if a change in the amount of memory occurs, try to correlate how it impacts performance. As with other testing, it is important to change only one thing at a time. If multiple changes take place it becomes difficult to determine which change impacted the performance and how.

Make only one change at a time and measure its impact on performance

Create a log of daily performance measurement which takes into account the factors mentioned above. It might look something like this:

Date _____   Test Cycle # _____

Test cycle description   _____

Number of users at the time of the test _____ _____

Client memory size _____   Server memory size _____

Client swapper file size _____   Server swapper file size _____

Network changes   _____

Application changes   _____

Database configuration changes   _____

Other notes   _____

Observation

Response time _____   Throughput _____   Utilization _____

Keeping track of this information will give you the data for baseline measurements. Without baseline data, comparisons to historical data cannot be made.

In summary, let's review some of the more important points:

- Start testing early. You have everything to gain and nothing to lose.

- Create a coherent, well thought-out plan for usability, regression, stress and performance testing.

- Speed up and improve testing with automated testing tools.

- Make testing as realistic as possible.

- Keep good records. Being able to reproduce a problem is the most important step to fixing it.

Suggested Reading

SQA:ROBOT User Guide, Lawrence, MA: Software Quality Automation, 1992. Contact SQA at (800) 228-9922.

13

Systems Management and
Deployment

If personal computers and workstations are so inexpensive, why are many companies finding out that distributed systems can actually cost more than mainframe-based systems? To find the answer, we must examine the total cost of ownership, not just the initial purchase price of hardware and software. In addition to the initial outlay, the total cost of ownership includes ongoing maintenance and support cost.

Distributed systems management is a large component of system costs

In the 1990s, the most expensive item is no longer the computer software or hardware. It is the cost of human labor that commands the highest premium. Salaries, benefits, rent, equipment purchases, travel, and unemployment insurance are just some of the items making the cost of labor very expensive. Since client/server projects today tend to be very human-intensive, it is not surprising that they cost more.

Human labor is very expensive

Distributed systems management—the day-to-day operational support of distributed systems—is a very human-intensive activity. Here are some reasons why:

Distributed systems management is labor intensive

- *Lack of good tools*   Simply put, there are very few tools available on the market today that can automate mundane administrative tasks, assist in problem determination and resolution, or help in capacity planning. The current selection of tools in the marketplace for the most part are a "release 1.0" generation and need time to mature. The client/server industry is still more focused on tools needed to build these applications, than on the tools needed for their operational support.

- *Inadequate organizational support structure*   While centralized systems management is well understood, distributed systems management is not. Many organizations are struggling to figure out how to organize themselves to support distributed applications. For example, one issue that often comes up is who is responsible for the day-to-day monitoring of such systems? Should it be the group that built the application or the glass house mainframe operations group?

Another issue that makes it difficult to decide how distributed systems should be supported and by whom is that they encompass many areas of technology. Should the group that built the system be responsible for the network, the operating system, the database, and other infrastructural components of the system?

- *Lack of knowledge and expertise*   As with many new technologies, the shortage of expertise is a significant obstacle to keeping costs down. A significant amount of money is being spent retraining the existing work force. In many situations, companies mistakenly add additional bodies to fix problems. Often times this *additional resource* type of mentality is actually counterproductive, because it is not the number of people that makes the problem go away, it is their experience and knowledge.

- *Lack of discipline and rigor in change management and problem management processes*   Many invaluable lessons must be learned by distributed systems administrators from their mainframe operations people. Mainframe operations discipline has evolved over the past thirty years to a very mature and established systems management process. From a user's point of view, the system uptime requirements do not change based on technology used. The biggest obstacle to such knowledge transfer is a cultural gap between the mainframe operations people and the PC generation.

The systems management process is similar to traditional systems management

Fundamentally, the process of distributed systems management is really not all that different from the traditional centralized systems management. It consists of the same basic subprocesses, namely, change management, problem management, performance management, and configuration management.

Change Management

As its name implies, a change management process has to do with managing any and all changes to the overall system. Such changes need to be carefully tracked, documented, and approved. Many studies have shown that well over 50% of system problems have occurred as a result of poorly planned changes made to a system. This also means that if there is a problem, chances are you can go back and examine the last couple of changes made to find its cause. I cannot emphasize enough the importance of a properly controlled change management process.

Many problems are attributed to changes applied to a system

A distributed system is an aggregation of many technologies: networking, database, operating system, GUI, and so on. Therefore, there is usually a team of specialists who support distributed systems. If your experience is anything like ours, you will find that as the number of people on the support team increases, making sure that good communication exists among all the players becomes a monumental task. And yet, good communication among all support team members is an absolute must, because anyone can introduce a change to a system that can negatively impact many other system components.

Distributed systems management is a team effort

For example, a network specialist might decide that too much RAM is allocated to the network interface card. He or she may decide that this resource needs to be reduced. The next day, the database server might not start, because it was configured to use a previously defined set of resources which are no longer available. Meanwhile the system would be down and 60 people in the office might not be able to get their work done! I could go through many examples like this that all point to one thing—that any system changes need to be carefully managed in a consensus driven, all-informed approach.

Lack of communication among the specialists can cause problems

To help with this task, start by creating a simple change management matrix. This matrix should consist of all products listed along one axis and various support groups listed along the other axis (Figure 13.1).

The change management matrix

Figure 13.1   Responsibility matrix

	Ethernet network	Transport protocol	Netware	DOS Windows UNIX	Sybase	Application development tools
Network support	R	A	A	A	N	
OS support	N	A	A	R	A	N
DBMS support	N	A	A	A	R	A
Network OS support	A	R	R	A	A	N
Help desk	N	N	N	N	N	N
Operations Control	N	N	N	N	N	N
Development support		N	N	A	A	A
Applications development		N	N	A	A	R

R = Responsible for support and change initiation
A = Must approve changes
N = Must be notified of changes

This matrix identifies roles and responsibilities

Each box of the matrix contains a letter which describes the typical role that a group is to play in the change management process. For example, the database support team must be notified of any changes in network topology, must also approve any changes in transport protocols, must approve operating system changes, is responsible for the database product support, and has the right to approve development tools.

A change management process must be devised

A change management process must be developed and institutionalizcd. It is not enough simply to devise the process and never use or reference it. Such a plan must be absorbed into organizational procedures.

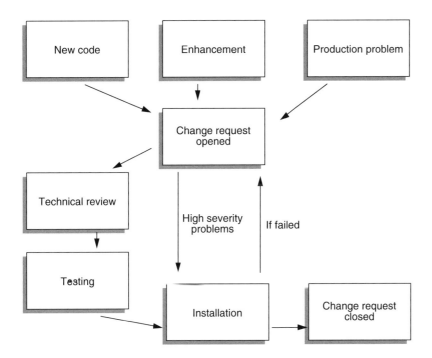

Figure 13.2   Change management process

In the sample change management plan in Figure 13.2, when a member of a support team wants to make a change, he or she must first open a change record in a change management database. A change record must specify:

A change management record captures pertinent information

- The reason for the proposed change

- The estimated impact

- The type of change: hardware, software, etc.

- Which component requires the change

Most changes, with the exception of severe production problems, must first be reviewed, approved, and tested. The process begins by notifying some groups and getting approval from others. Subsequently, any proposed change must first be tested in a lab environment. Only after successful testing should a change be made to a production system. This process ensures that all changes made to a system will be consensus driven, and are more like to be technically sound. Most importantly, they will be communicated to and understood by all of the groups involved in distributed systems support.

Changes must be tested and approved

All change management processes have common goals

Your organization might have a slightly different version of a change management process; nevertheless, any change management process must:

- Ensure that changes are technically sound

- Be documented where it can be accessed by all support personnel

- Be verified in a lab setting

- Be scheduled according to the needs of the business and be sensitive to various business activities

- Keep everyone who is part of the process informed at all times

- Ensure management involvement and approval of the process (buy-in)

- Have change back-out procedures available

Change management is often perceived as burdensome

At first glance such a process may seem too cumbersome or bureaucratic, but without it a high availability of systems cannot be guaranteed. The financial savings alone derived from increased system availability and reduction in support calls will justify any additional time spent on intragroup communication.

Much can be done to automate the process

Of course, much can be done to make the change management process less painful. By using e-mail with predefined distribution lists or a simple change management system which keeps track of changes made and the state of proposed changes, the change management process can become much less burdensome.

Acceptance Testing Lab

An acceptance testing lab is a must when the stakes are high

Even when there is good communication among support team members, the smallest change made to a system in production can bring the system down. When a distributed system is down, possibly hundreds of people can be impacted, costing the company a significant amount of money through lost business and an idle work force. To many companies, this is simply unacceptable. One way to make sure that such downtime is minimized is to create an acceptance testing laboratory. The goal of this lab is to replicate as closely as possible the company's production environment.

The idea is very simple—first introduce a change in the acceptance lab to see if any system problems will arise. Only after the system has been used to perform all of its usual tasks can the change be made in the real production setting. A good way to quickly run through system tests is to use an automated test tool (which, hopefully, was used during testing). By simulating user keyboard actions, such tools can quickly achieve broad coverage of system functions.

Use automated system tools

There are several simple guidelines that must be followed in an acceptance testing laboratory:

Acceptance lab guidelines

- All computers must be configured *identically or at the very least as closely as possible* to those in the production environment. The idea here is to keep the number of differences between the acceptance and production environments to an absolute minimum. Otherwise, if differences exist, more problems are likely to slip through the cracks.

- The acceptance laboratory must be controlled. It should not be a place for doing ad hoc changes or other kinds of unscheduled testing. Configurations of all machines in the lab must be consistent at all times. Any variation can increase the chance of a problem slipping into the production environment.

Whether your company needs an acceptance laboratory is a purely financial decision. If the nature of your business is such that even a small system outage results in a substantial business loss, an acceptance lab will easily pay for itself.

An acceptance lab must be cost justified

Problem Management

No matter how much testing gets done in a laboratory environment, some problems are bound to escape undetected into production. Therefore, a problem management discipline must be developed in order to effectively deal with these situations.

Problem management should be a structured process

Problem information must be captured as close to the source as possible

The first and foremost requirement to problem solving is having good and complete information. Good information is needed to make an accurate diagnosis and quickly resolve a problem. Such information needs to be collected as close to the source of the problem as possible. The more people who participate in the information gathering process, the higher the likelihood of misinformation creeping in. You probably remember the game *telephone* that children play. A story is passed on from person to person, and usually it has changed completely by the time it gets to the last person. My point here is that a message can change dramatically while in transit. This is only human!

Problem information must be accessible to everyone involved

To minimize misinformation, all problem-related information must be captured by the first support person that comes into contact with the problem. It must be recorded on a system that is accessible to everyone who is likely to get involved in the resolution of this problem.

What sort of information is important in resolving problems for distributed systems? The short answer is *everything*. The form below can be used as a starting point.

Time _____   Date _____   Severity _____

Person reporting the problem _____   Location _____

Problem description _____

_____

_____

Application/system name _____

Hardware platform _____

Operating system version number _____

Operating system revision level _____

Transport protocol _____   Revision level _____

DBMS _____   Revision level _____

Record of action (when /who/action) _____

_____

_____

A good problem management system not only retains problem information, but also manages it effectively. For example, many mundane things like making sure that the person having a problem is using the right level of software should be done by the system automatically. Another useful feature of a well thought-out problem management system is when it can search through open problem records and identify those that might be related to the problem at hand. It should also allow its users to quickly examine any recent changes made to the system.

Good problem management systems do a lot of work for you

Finally, such a system must keep the problem management process moving. It should flag problems that have been outstanding past their allowed resolution time and notify appropriate management.

Problems must be tracked

The Problem Management Process

Before a problem management system is put in place, a company must develop a problem management process. The goal of this process is to clearly define a set of steps and procedures that should be followed. It should start when a problem gets reported and follow the problem through until its final resolution. The following diagram (Figure 13.3) depicts how a problem resolution process might work. This diagram shows the help desk as the first contact for the user. The person on the help desk should be sufficiently trained to:

A problem management process is a set of rules and procedures

- Understand problem information (and its technical details) to be able to correctly capture it on the system

- Be able to separate user errors from real problems, thus successfully closing a large number of reported problems

- Determine a user's educational gaps and advise on how to remedy them

If the problem is indeed real, it is assigned to a specialist. He or she must assume responsibility for seeing the problem through until it is resolved. Without a single person assuming problem ownership, the process usually gets stuck in Never-Never land, leaving the user feeling frustrated.

Someone must become the problem manager

Figure 13.3 Problem management process

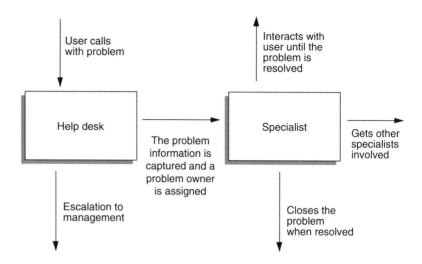

Specialists must be encouraged to cooperate

A single person can't know all the technologies involved in distributed computing. He or she must be able to draw on the knowledge of others. Such cooperation between specialists must be encouraged and rewarded.

A problem management process must be measured

A successful problem management process must include some form of measurement. It is simply not enough to assume that the process is working efficiently. Collecting important metrics about the process, such as the average time needed to resolve problems and frequent sources of problems, can be used to improve the overall quality of the software and correctly identify system expenses to the business.

Disaster Recovery Procedures

Plan for disaster!

A vital component of a problem management process is disaster recovery. A disaster recovery plan must be well thought out and tested so that when (and not if) Murphy's Law strikes again, a company will be able to get back on track quickly and painlessly.

Identify points of failure and desired recovery times

The first step in a disaster recovery plan is to understand your users' needs. The basic premise is to identify all of the possible points of failure and to decide on the amount of time needed to restore the system. What kinds of things can go wrong? There is certainly no shortage of items on that list. These are just a few to get you started:

- *Hardware failures*   System, disk drive, network cards, etc.

- *Software failures*   Operating system, DBMS, file server, abnormal application termination, etc.

- *Natural disasters*   Flood, hurricane, fire, etc.

Once such potential problems are identified, the next step is to review them with your users. Only the users can specify what impact a system outage will have on the bottom line of the business. Then, jointly, you can discuss what solutions are available and whether they can be cost justified.

Cost justify the proposed solution

A disaster recovery plan must specifically outline every type of possible outage and how long the recovery will take. Here again, you must seek your users' guidance to determine if the plan is reasonable from a business point of view. Of course, with an unlimited budget every system condition can be taken care of, but in the real world that's not what happens. In order to decide how to wisely spend your system recovery dollars, you and your users need to determine the level of recovery that is needed.

Users must be involved

Writing a disaster recovery plan and putting it on the shelf is not enough. A disaster recovery plan must be tested. Try to simulate possible problems to see if the plan is based on valid assumptions. This *fire drill* exercise will help you add a dimension of realism to your plan and help raise the overall level of confidence in your system.

A disaster recovery plan must be tested

Now let's examine some of the processes, standards, and tools that automate systems management.

Software Distribution

One of the most difficult tasks in distributed systems management is software distribution. The basic question here that needs to be answered is: "How will the software be distributed initially to possibly hundreds of computers and how will the subsequent software fixes be applied?" If your system will consist of 20 users located in a single geographic location this task is manageable using a sneakernet method. However, if the solution involves hundreds of users located in many cities, a software distribution strategy must be devised.

The software distribution challenge grows as the number of users increases

Software distribution is ranked as the top obstacle

Many early adapters of client/server technology have ranked the software distribution as the number one obstacle that they had to overcome. There are several solutions to this challenging problem:

Set up a master server

- *File server-based distribution*   This approach assumes that all users are connected to a local area network that spans multiple geographic locations. Another prerequisite is that a file server exists at every user site. The idea is simple. Designate one file server to be the master file server for your application. Every new release and all code fixes will be stored there first.

Distribute changed files from there to all other servers

The master server should have access to other file servers located in the field offices. When a change is made to the master file server, it should automatically trigger a routine that copies the new version to all field office servers. To start this application, write a simple batch file that first compares the dates of executable modules on a user machine with those on the file server. If the dates do not match, copy the file server version to a local drive and then start the application (Figure 13.4).

Figure 13.4   File server-based software distribution

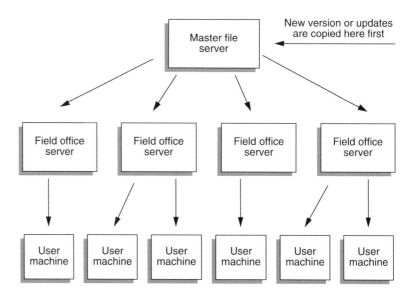

This approach is simple, but problematic

The advantage of this approach is its simplicity. There is no need to buy any additional software, and the batch files can be written fairly quickly. Unfortunately, there are also several disadvantages. First of all, this approach is difficult to measure and control. For example, there is no way to check from a central location what version of software the user is on. There is no track record of what has been distributed.

Second, having to potentially copy new files when the user starts the system could be a nuisance in terms of the time involved in copying the files. That is especially true if an application consists of many large files.

It can interfere with user tasks

Third, this method lacks a *push* capability. An administrator cannot decide to immediately push the files to all user machines. Instead, this method relies on a user's *pull* to distribute the software. Ideally, a push-and-pull approach is desirable.

It relies on user actions

- *Software distribution tools* There are a number of tools available today that can mass distribute software directly to any machine on the network. One machine is designated to be a master console, and controls the scheduling of software distribution updates. Most such tools make use of software *agents* that run on every user machine (Figure 13.5). Agents are programs that communicate on a peer-to-peer basis with the master console.

A number of more sophisticated solutions use workstation agents

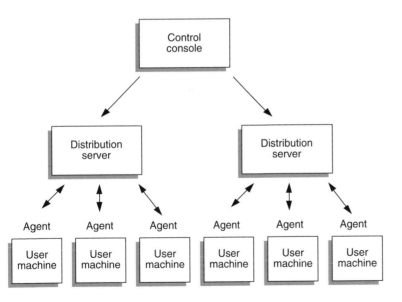

Figure 13.5 Software distribution tool

| | This means that either an agent or the console can initiate software distribution. This is how the push-and-pull method is accomplished. The pull method is agent driven. If an agent running on a user's machine discovers that the software on that machine needs upgrading, it can request (pull) a newer version from a master console. The push approach is driven by the master console. Upgrades are distributed (pushed) to all machines that have been designated for the software. |

A push-and-pull approach is now possible

This means that either an agent or the console can initiate software distribution. This is how the push-and-pull method is accomplished. The pull method is agent driven. If an agent running on a user's machine discovers that the software on that machine needs upgrading, it can request (pull) a newer version from a master console. The push approach is driven by the master console. Upgrades are distributed (pushed) to all machines that have been designated for the software.

Agents can perform many tasks

Software agents running on every user machine also can do configuration management. A master console can direct a software agent to check any user's operating system version, the amount of disk space available, or to perform virtually any other task.

Protocol Analyzers

Protocol analyzers are indispensable to network support groups

Another very useful tool for any organization using distributed systems is a protocol analyzer. A more common name for this is a *network sniffer,* which was the name of the original network protocol analyzer from Network General. Protocol analyzers can be used to:

- Trace network traffic by capturing all or some of the data between workstations (Figure 13.6). This is especially useful when it comes to verifying connectivity, verifying data transmission, and verifying the amount of data sent.

Figure 13.6 Network frame as decoded by a network traffic analyzer

Frame type	Transport protocol header	Application level protocols	Data
Token ring or Ethernet	TCP, IPX NetBIOS	SMB, Named Pipes, FTP	

- Measure the time spent in transit on the network between any two nodes. This is helpful in tracking down performance problems.

- Spot network congestion before major problems develop.

- Help you understand the inner workings of transport protocols so that you can write your software to use the network more efficiently.

There are many protocol analyzers on the market today. All of them basically offer similar functionality. When purchasing a network analyzer, make sure that its interface is easy to use. Figuring out how to set various filtering options should not require the user to be a brain surgeon. Another distinguishing characteristic of a good network analyzer is data interpretation. It should not only display the data in their raw form, but also help you interpret them. To a novice user of a network protocol analyzer, that would help tremendously.

A good protocol analyzer should help you interpret the data

Network Management

As networks grew larger and more complex, it became obvious that managing them required tools that could isolate network problems and would be able to take corrective actions. It also became apparent that a standard was needed for network management in a heterogeneous network. Wire-level problems, bridges, routers, network interface cards all can be managed if they support a common management protocol.

Network management is focused on infrastructure management

In today's networks, the most popular network management protocol is the *simple network management protocol* (SNMP). SNMP grew up on the Internet. SNMP divides the network into managers and managed devices. A manager is typically a high-powered workstation with a GUI interface. It acts as a network controller by sending out commands (or PDUs in SNMP jargon) to managed devices. A managed device can be a bridge, a network interface card, a wiring concentrator, or any other device with networking capability. To be managed, a device must run an agent which communicates with a managing station.

SNMP is a popular network management protocol

Figure 13.7 SNMP-based monitoring

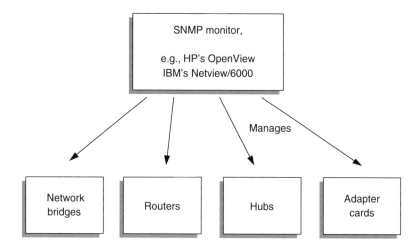

There are a number of SNMP products in use

The most popular SNMP-based network managers today are HP's OpenView and Sun's SunNet Manager. Both products have now been on the market for several years and offer friendly user and programming interfaces. To understand how these products work, we must first take a closer look at how SNMP works. An SNMP agent is responsible for managing a network device, but what does the word *manage* really mean?

Every network device has some important information that controls its operation

Every network device internally stores some form of configuration data. For example, a network interface card typically contains information about the network speed, the interrupt number used for communication with the CPU, send and receive buffer sizes and their locations, etc. To manage, that is, to be able to change any of this information, an agent must be able to access it from the card at any time. There must be some means for capturing this information in a consistent way regardless of the type of network device used.

It is stored in MIBs

This is a function of a *management information base* (MIB). A MIB is a hierarchical collection of definitions of what amounts to variables that can be read and written to. In an MIB language these variables are called *objects*. Each object has a name, syntax, and value. The various commands are performed on the objects by an agent (Figure 13.8).

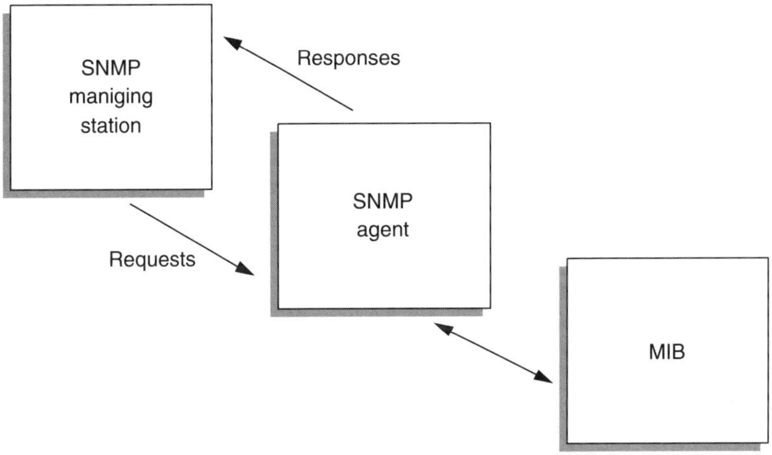

Figure 13.8 SNMP information flow

In terms of information flow, SNMP is indeed a simple protocol. The SNMP standard defines only the five commands that are summarized in the following table.

SNMP defines only five commands

SNMP Commands	Description
GetRequest	Used by the manager station to query agents on the status of objects.
GetNextRequest	Like GetRequest, this function steps through the MIB one entry at a time (sequentially).
SetRequest	This is how a manager directs a change in the status of a managed object.
GetResponse	Forces agent to answer GetRequest.
Trap	Agent notifies a manager that a significant event has occurred.

SNMP has recently been upgraded to SNMP V2. SNMP V2 extends the original standard, but preserves many original concepts for a smooth migration.

An Alternative to SNMP

CMIP is another competing standard

SNMP has a competitor. This standard, defined by the OSI, is called CMIP, which stands for *Common Management Information Protocol*. CMIP has been used mostly in telecommunications, but has not made much presence in the LAN and WAN environments. An often cited reason is the additional overhead needed to run CMIP.

SNMP's limitations

Which standard is better is largely a matter of opinion. From a user's point of view, it is the function provided by a network management tool that really matters. Each standard has advantages and disadvantages. For example, SNMP has a number of limitations:

- For SNMP to work, the network must be up and running. It seems to be an oxymoron that a solution to network problems requires a properly operating network.

- SNMP agents are sometimes difficult to install and configure. This is a manual process, which on a large network can become time consuming.

- SNMP, for the most part, ignores other important management components such as the operating system, processors, and user-written applications.

SNMP is a good solution

Although SNMP does not solve all problems, today it is still the best solution for resolving network-related problems.

Distributed Systems Management

Distributed systems management covers systems level components

The term *distributed systems management* is relatively new. It refers to managing the system level components of a distributed system, such as operating systems and database management systems. For example, it would be really useful to know the utilization of a processor on any computer in the network at a given time, or to find out if a DBMS on the server machine has deadlocked.

There is still a long way to go

Ideally, a system administrator should be able to query and set any parameter in any system component running on any computer in the network. The reality of the situation is much more modest.

A number of distributed systems management tools have emerged primarily in the UNIX world. One such tool from Tivoli Systems automates some user administration tasks. For example, it simplifies the addition and removal of user ids, schedules system maintenance activities, starts and stops applications, and performs other useful tasks.

Example of a tool

Tivoli Systems' framework for distributed systems management has been chosen by OSF's DME project as the primary model. With uncertainty surrounding DME, the distributed systems management industry is unlikely to see any wide scale standards emerging in the very near future. Therefore, from a practical perspective the buyer would do best by searching for tools that offer desired functionality.

Industry standards are not here yet

Distributed systems management tools are beginning to appear on non-UNIX platforms as well. IBM, for example, has launched a very ambitious distributed systems management effort for OS/2. IBM's strategy consists of a family of products called LAN Netview. Similar to its mainframe cousin, LAN Netview products allow the system administration to:

IBM's strategy

- View the network in terms of user machines and servers

- Monitor and change parameters in various system components

- Perform basic troubleshooting

- Better perform asset and configuration management

- Distribute software and software changes throughout the network

For the most part, LAN Netview has fallen short on deliverables. At the time of this writing, it appears that IBM has gone back to the drawing board to rethink its strategy.

IBM's systems management offerings have fallen short

Microsoft has recently entered the distributed systems market with a systems management server (SMS) tool code named *Hermes*. This tool will focus on software distribution, remote troubleshooting, software licensing and metering, and software inventory on Windows and Windows NY systems. Microsoft realizes that unless desktop management issues are addressed, further transition to client/server computing at the enterprise level will be difficult.

Microsoft will be an important player in the distributed systems management market

Conclusion

Distributed systems management is serious business

Systems management often takes a back seat to systems development, and yet operational support is just as important to successful distributed systems delivery. Even the most elegantly designed distributed systems can fail because they can be impossible to manage and maintain. Keep in mind that such failures can impact tens and hundreds of users, and cost companies millions of dollars in lost business and productivity. We must not forget the lessons already learned in established mainframe operations. Following is a checklist designed to determine your organization's readiness for distributed systems support.

1   Has a support group been identified for your applications?

2   Do they have the skills needed to maintain the system?

3   What tools will be used to aid in administration, problem determination, and problem tracking?

4   Has a problem management process been established and reviewed with its users?

5   Has a change management process been identified and automated?

6   Is there a tested and proven disaster recovery plan?

7   How will the software be installed and distributed to its users?

8   Have all possible areas of automation been examined?

Suggested Reading

Desktop Management Interface Specification 1.0, Desktop Management Task Force, Portland: Intel Corporation, 1994.

Marshall Rose, *The Simple Book,* Englewood Cliffs: Prentice Hall, 1994.

"Networked Systems Management: Managing the New Computing Models," Gartner Group briefing, 1993. Gartner Group can be reached at (203) 967-6700 voice, or (203) 967-6191 fax.

Index

IP 67
IPX/SPX 71, 72, 75, 76, 82, 91, 97

L

labor expense 29
LAN 16, 57, 62
LAN application 16
LAN Manager 91, 92
LAN Server 91–93
Lantastic 92
laser printer 25
layer 60
locking scheme 15
lost business opportunity 37
LUW 77

M

mainframe data center 25
MAN 58
management information base 218
management objective 21
management support 9
management task 17
marketectures 160
media independence 67
memory mapped file 86
method 170
methodology 165
MIB 218
Microsoft LAN Manager 3, 57
middleware, see *database middleware*
Mirroring 108
modem 90
Mozart 111, 134
MS Excel 28
MS-DOS 81, 82
MS-Windows 84
multiple physical databases 14
multiple sites 17, 19
multiprotocol networking 82
multitasking 82, 83, 86

N

NCB 76, 148
NetBIOS 72, 82, 92, 97, 147
    command 147, 148
    programming 148
NetWare 5, 72, 75, 91, 93
NetWare Lite 92
network 16
    analyzer 28
    card 25
    connection 15
    control block 148
    layer 66
    operating system 26, 27, 70, 89–92
    sniffer 216
    speed 16
    traffic 16
    transparency 90
Notes 121–124
Notes server 5
Novell 91
Novell Netware 57
NT 82, 88, 93

O

object-oriented analysis and design 167
objects 170
ObjectView 110, 111
ODBC 98
OLE 51
OLTP 143
ongoing support 30
on-line backups 108
OOA/OOD 167, 169
Open Data Services 109
operating system 26, 81, 88, 89
operational support 19
Oracle 103, 145
OS/2   82, 86, 88, 93, 160
OSF 221
OSI 71, 77–79
OSI model 59

P

page 87
painter 111
Paradox 38
peer-to-peer 7, 38, 92
performance testing 197, 198
   mechanics of 198
personal computer 25, 33, 88
physical design 16
physical I/O 86
PL/1   110
polymorphism 181
PowerBuilder 110–113, 158, 159, 160, 178
presentation layer 78
presentation space 136
process 84, 86, 87, 107
processor-to-I/O access speed 16
processor-to-memory access speed 16
product support 45
programming interface 70
protocol analyzer 216, 217

R

RAM 88
redirected drive model 156
redirection 89, 90
referential integrity 109
regression testing 191
relational database 95
remote application control 17
remote data management model 155, 179
remote interface model 140
remote procedure call 131
remote request 161
remote unit of work 162
response time 198
responsibility 172
RIPL 93
robustness 88
roll-forward recovery 108
roll-out strategy 53
router 68
routing 66

S

scalability 18
screen scraping 134
security 82, 88
segment 87
select 95
semaphore 87
sequel 95
server 93
   accessory 25
   component 91
   machine 25
   programmer 52
session 75
session layer 77
shielded twisted pair 62
simple network management protocol (SNMP) 217, 219, 220
skill 12
small law office, example 37
Smalltalk 131
SNA 59, 72
software distribution 17, 24
software distribution tool 27
software maintenance cost 29
software testing tool 29
SPX 75–77
SQA:Robot 192, 193
SQL 95, 104, 144–147, 152
SQL Access Group 98
SQL Server 93, 108
SQLWindows 110, 111, 158, 159, 178
static SQL 104
stored procedure 106
stored procedures 144
stress testing 194
support 24
support group 30
support organization 32
Sybase 102, 103, 108, 144, 145, 147
synchronization 78
syncpoints 78
system size 15
systems administrator 53
systems management tool 27

T

technical architect 49
thinness 129
third generation language (3GL) 52, 115, 116, 160
thread 82, 84–87, 107
threads 82, 84
throughput 198
Tivoli Systems 221
token ring network 16, 63–65, 128
TP Monitor 89
traditional programmer 51
traffic pattern 16
training 24
transaction 15, 83, 144
transaction oriented system 13
transaction program 78
Transact-SQL 109, 144–147
Transmission Control Protocol/Internet Protocol
 (TCP/IP) 70–72, 82, 92, 97
transport layer 69, 70
transport protocol 96
trigger 106, 109
two-phase commit protocol 14

U

Uniface 178
UNIX 71, 72, 81, 82, 93, 156, 179, 180, 221
unshielded twisted pair 62
update 95
user 17, 33
user interface/human factors consultant 51
utilization 198

V

vendor's alliance 43
vendor's support 45
Vines 91
virtual circuit 75
virtual LAN 16
virtual memory management 82, 87
Visual Basic 110
VMS 81, 82
VSAM 99

W

watchdog 76
wide area link 16
wide area network (WAN) 16, 58
Windows 86
Windows for Workgroups 92
wiring 25
word processing 38
workflow management 120
workflow system 120
workstation 88

X

X Window 140, 141, 143, 177, 179
Xerox 91